All's Well.

John Lefebvre

All's Well.

WHERE THOU ART EARTH

AND WHY

L

John Lefebvre Press
Salt Spring Island, BC
johnlefebvre.com

Cataloguing data available from Library and Archives Canada
ISBN 978-0-9959042-3-1 (hardcover)
ISBN 978-0-9959042-0-0 (paperback)
ISBN 978-0-9959042-1-7 (ebook)

Produced by Page Two
www.pagetwostrategies.com
Editing by Shirarose Wilensky
Cover and interior design by Peter Cocking
Cover and endpapers illustrations by Michelle Clement
Illustrations adapted from original work by Trevor Cook
Printed and bound in Canada by Friesens

IMAGE CREDITS:
Image 1: *Wren*, photo by Geoff Savage, 2015.
Image 2: Bronze sword, 15th century BCE, Sumer, with *Liberty*, bronze female figure from Amsterdam, 2004. Photo by Geoff Savage, 2017.
Image 3: *Liberty*, bronze sculpture from Amsterdam, 2004. Photo by Geoff Savage, 2017.
Image 4: *Sea Do*, ink and watercolor by Donna Wenkoff, 2012.
Image 5: *Couple Looking Out In Space*, terracotta by Charles Breth, 2005. Photo by Geoff Savage, 2017.

Theresa Louise Lefebvre, born not long after Earth

began to go around the Sun, and when she died,

there were half a trillion galaxies and a multiverse.

Who taught the three most powerful things were faith,

hope and charity, but the greatest of these is love.

Contents

Plotting the Wages of Nice

It only takes Simple Arithmetic for us to plot sufficiently our place in infinity and in eternity. Where we stand compared to our ideals is less easily contrived.

CERTAIN EVENTS in my life, I concede,
may seem extraordinary, but if they were,
I think it was only in a small way. Although
I stumbled upon fabulous wealth and had all that
I wanted—and much more—of what our world
can sell us, the *most* astonishing things that
have befallen me fell into my lap no more than
they have into anyone's.

Still, when you quit the law to busk on
street corners, then strike it rich on Internet
gambling, lend friends your places on the beach
in Malibu and the private jet to get there, get
arrested by Uncle Sam, then record with the
best studio musicians in America while out on

$5 million bail, the story seems fantastic and people think you should write it. So I began, but very quickly tired of writing sentences that started with "I" and ended with "me." The rags-to-riches literature is one to which I did not wish to make a contribution. It's not that the story was lurid; lurid needs to be told, too. Perhaps it was just the meaninglessness of such stories, the perpetuation of questionable materialist dreams and the cultivation of almost certain disappoint-ment. And so I decided to leave the telling of tall tales to others.

Still again, I do have a story to tell, and as it turns out, there can be no story more lurid. It is the story of us all.

"The story of us all?"

Yes. Indeed, it is one from which we might learn smart lessons and, on that account alone, much more worth the telling. Perhaps the best way to start may be to look at who we are now, where we have come. We may see a lot more about where we have been by looking at what we have made of ourselves.

If lurid stories have no other redeeming value, at least they immerse us in moral quandaries that might challenge our own assumptions. Per-haps in the end they may point us toward more fairness and greater wisdom. For instance, many, having taken an honest look at current world culture, might shake their heads in wonder and possibly even gain some sympathy for Western world leaders like Barack Obama.

Until now, America's presidents have been elected only on such narrow moral prerequisites that 90 percent of the people in my graduating class wouldn't make the cut. First, they had to profess a profound commitment to our biblical God at His most hard-boiled, and failing that, they may as well have taken their religious freedom for a permanent hike.

Then, a president must step into the wilds and deal with the powerful, selfish bastards of the world on all sides. When it looks like there might be a case of "us or them," they must neutralize the threat, on their way into Christian church, with drones. You have to feel some sympathy for their dilemma. Either Jesus had not considered this circumstance while formulating his lessons of pure love, or somehow, killing pricks is an act of Christ-like compassion.

That has all changed now, though even President Trump felt the need to allegate, "I will be the greatest jobs president that God ever created." But he personates himself plainly. More than enough about him already. Now the evangelical right clearly demonstrates an underlying strangeness of morality. Where Jesus of Nazareth proclaimed loving all and, foremost, loving mostly the least among us all, self-proclaimed Christians now pervert Jesus' words to support anti-gay, anti-black, anti-Muslim, anti-woman, anti-liberal screed, all the while literally turning their backs upon all the poorest in our world, three-quarters of Earth's population, in advancement of their own selfish comfort.

Who can resist a tale, no matter how tawdry, that leads us somewhere like this: Christ sanctioning white supremacy, disregarding the poor and dealing with our enemies by neutralization with extreme prejudice?

When the low story of the high life is our own, then pesky considerations arise. The most challenging might be whether we can demonstrate having learned lessons—high or not—honestly enough to properly honor having had the lessons in the first place. Obama has got to be a different kind of Christian after serving as president, compared to, for example, his predecessor or Dick Cheney, who seemed to be different kinds of Christians even before their service started. What have we learned from these and our other teachers, and from our own experience—the lessons we were taught? Or the ones we are shown?

Too many of the lessons that we were taught as kids turned out to be delusion, if not hypocrisy. Elders and persons in authority are entitled to respect. The West is the champion of freedom. Rich and poor are exactly equal in a democracy: one person, one vote. Unbridled free enterprise is best and fairest for everybody. Money is safe with bankers. Nothing travels faster than the speed of light. We are unique in the Universe.

Many more lessons were undeniably right but exist if at all only as ideals. Equal justice under law. Propaganda comes only from the likes of fascists or communists. The media in the West tell the truth. Don't bully. Liars are not rewarded. It is better to give than to receive. Clean up after yourself. Leave the world a better place. Good cowboys look out for the little guys. Human rights for all.

And where have these lessons, for what they are worth, left us?

One thing we know for certain is the thing we avoid considering the most. Soon we will all be dead. Then we will be succeeded in our tenancy here by others of us. What will our successors know that we do not? What will they realize that we have not?

How do we contend with the astonishing natural bounty that has befallen us? How do we understand the disconnect between our ideals and our gifts on the one hand and our actual accomplishments and behaviors on the other? Do we carefully consider what we can say we know and what we cannot? Here we are out of the caves 150 generations, enjoying prosperity beyond anybody's dreams, and while we celebrate freedom in our lives daily, we are unable or unwilling to prevent mass deprivation and abasement of our kind all over Earth.

How does our story, the true story of us all, measure up to the tales we've been told, that we tell ourselves still and, unblinkingly, pass on? How do we measure up as the guardians of freedom and the other democratic values we proclaim to uphold? Or to the wisdom of religious and other moral leaders that we exalt?

It only takes Simple Arithmetic for us to plot sufficiently our place in infinity and in eternity. Where we stand compared to our ideals is less easily contrived.

Simple Arithmetic can also prove that we are on the brink of an advance in wealth and knowledge vastly exceeding what has ever been dreamt by any of us.

The part that will inspire the most sniggers is this: the only thing we need do to get there is be nice.

1

Misconceptions: The Short History of Our Learning

Ironically, over the last two hundred years or so, about three startled blinks in our history, this understanding of our fallibility has brought us our steepest learning curve ever, by far.

DAVID DEUTSCH is an Oxford University quantum physicist and quantum computing theorist. In his recent book, *The Beginning of Infinity*, he presents his home field with uncondescending sensibleness and takes us on an audacious rollick through the unfolding of our species and of life generally, our physical and cultural development, and our accumulated collective knowledge.

Deutsch asks that we imagine for a moment the accumulation and progress of human learning as an ever-increasing funnel of collective knowledge. If we sliced a cross section at any given point, we would find a state of affairs where people thought they had just about everything figured out. Of course, in this, they were always wrong—most often, exceedingly.

So often have we been caught out with our knowledge incomplete, if not completely wrong, that we take it for granted now, for the first time in our history, that some of our explanations are not yet as good as they should be. Now it is becoming more common that our explanations—old or new—are vigorously reconsidered in the light of new information.

This point of view, introduced by philosopher Karl Popper, Deutsch calls fallibilism, the awareness that, *always*, some of our explanations are not yet the best they can be. And so he proposes that rather than calling new scientific explanations "theories," we call them "misconceptions" from the start—the General Misconception of Relativity—and get on with finding out what is incorrect about them.

To improve our knowledge and to refine our explanations, we must first question what we *think* we know, and then find out what we *do not*.

Ironically, over the last two hundred years, about three startled blinks in our history, this understanding of our fallibility has brought us our steepest learning curve ever, by far. Both the quantity and quality of our knowledge are growing rapidly, and at a rapidly accelerating rate.

We have learned wonderful things from the

past. One of them is that most of what we thought we knew was wrong. Another is how much we do not know yet. What can we learn from the future? One hundred years from now exists. We know some things about it—for example, that our population will be more than 10 billion. A thousand years from now exists. What will we know then that we do not know now?

We know things unfold in systems with patterns, and the more the patterns emerge, the better we may anticipate our future. In his 2013 book, MIT senior lecturer Otto Scharmer speaks of learning from "the emerging future." Public relations expert Jim Hoggan provides a great introduction to this concept in *I'm Right and You're an Idiot*. There are few things about which we may be certain, but one of them is that our future will be built mostly upon new knowledge.

What will we learn from our emerging future? What on Earth are we? What are we doing? And what else might we be doing? Only there, in our future, may we discover, embrace and implement our better explanations—the sooner, the better.

Just one more matter of housekeeping. I suggest we call our planet "Earth," and not, please, "the earth." Okay, it's only a style thing, but, "the earth?" Maybe it just sounds a bit like "the wife." "The Donald." Maybe "the" removes us from her a bit. "The mom."

2

Simple Facts and All Likelihood— Not Alone, Just Lonely

We think that, among that many stars, so many that it would take seven Big Bangs to call out all their names, if we called roll, still from only one would we hear, "Present."

WHEN MY MOTHER was born, in 1927, we had hardly realized yet that our Sun was just another star. We did not know there was a difference between a star and a galaxy, only that some stars looked a bit fuzzy.

Now, ninety years later, we know staggeringly more. The Universe is neither static nor collapsing, but it is expanding, and at an accelerating rate. With extremely sensitive radio telescopes, we have identified and begun to understand exotic quasars and pulsars hundreds of millions and billions of light-years away. We "see" light that is 16 billion light-years away, knowing that is exactly the same as saying the light is from 16 billion years ago, probably remnants of a Big Bang. We don't "see" black holes, but we know they are there, immeasurably massive, at the very hearts of galaxies. For black holes, gravity is our eyes.

We know that our galaxy, the Milky Way, is more or less average in size and contains about 250 billion stars. And now we know that there are several hundreds of billions of galaxies. Recent estimates suggest even 400 billion galaxies in the visible universe, many of them vastly bigger than ours.

What does it mean that there are 400 billion galaxies, each with a few hundred billion stars? With Simple Arithmetic, we may begin plotting our positions in infinity and eternity, in "the scheme of things," as they say. I ask those of you who do not feel quite at home with math to be a bit carefree and think not so much about arithmetic as about general comparisons of extent and scale.

400 billion galaxies × 250 billion stars = 100 sextillion stars.

Yes. Sextillion. Or, in other words:
400,000,000,000 galaxies ×
250,000,000,000 stars =
100,000,000,000,000,000,000,000 stars.

That is one hundred thousand million-million-millions of stars.

I find vast numbers easier to contemplate when rendered as Image.

Take sugar.

If every star in the Universe were a sugar cube, the sugar cubes would be over our heads across all land on Earth. All the land you've ever flown over, and all the rest, every sports field, golf course, ski hill or city, all farmland, forests, mountain ranges and continents, six feet deep in sugar cubes.

Of course, even that analogy is like saying 100 sextillion is too vast to imagine. But I think it is not *that* vast, even for us.

Let's try words in a book.

If each star in our Milky Way galaxy were named in a book, the book would be thirty-two miles thick. You could read the equivalent of a popular novel each day, but it would still take 14,269 years to read each of the names of all the stars in our single galaxy.

If every galaxy in our Universe were named, that book would be fifty-three miles thick, eight times higher than Mount Everest is above sea level. It would take 22,830 years to read the names of all of the galaxies in the Universe.

But the names of every star in every galaxy in the Universe would fill a book that goes around Earth's equator 10,380 times, and it would take

115 billion years to read every name. (Speed readers may get it under 100 billion years.)

Cosmologists now estimate that about 16 billion years have passed since a Big Bang. If you had been reading out stars' names since that Big Bang, you would still have six more Big Bangs to go before you had read the names of all the stars in the Universe.

Between Google and a cell phone calculator, any fourth grade kid can check my arithmetic.

And what on Earth do we *think* of this? I'm a member of a self-ordained intelligent species that thinks itself alone in a universe that we, only a hundred years ago, did not even know existed. As members of this group, we call ourselves Human Beings. We think that, among that many stars, so many that it would take seven Big Bangs to call out each of their names, if we called roll, still from only one would we hear, "Present."

Our most imaginative argument in support of our uniqueness meme is that we've never heard from anybody. As if anybody could possibly know how to get in touch with us, but for some reason, would not bother.

If you are reading this, I'll have to allow that you're probably one of us Human Beings too, because, at least for now, I'm prepared to give you that the chances of this book having some wider audience than just humans on Earth, though vastly compelling, have yet to be granted.

But what are my chances of having such a wider audience?

The Misconception of 10 Trillion

Twenty-five thoughtful species in each of 400 billion galaxies equals 10 trillion thoughtful species in the Universe.

IF WHAT has occurred on Earth, the existence of creatures with approximately the awareness level of Human Beings, is a 1-in-250-billion chance, there must be one more species like us in every other galaxy, more or less.

That would be 400 billion more species like us in the Universe. For now, let's call that the Misconception of 400 Billion because I'm afraid that *that* number is laughably low.

Let's see.

The Misconception of 400 Billion is predicated upon the assumption that thoughtful life occurs only once in every 250 billion stars. Yet our empirical experience is that wherever we have come across a planet with large amounts of liquid surface water, there exists thoughtful life in *every* case. Ours.

If the chances of finding planets with liquid surface water are one in a million stars, then there are 250,000 such watery planets in our galaxy. I would bet that the chances are more like one in 10,000, which would mean there are 25 million such watery planets in our galaxy alone. However that may be, time will tell.

But let us return to what we know for certain. Probably our empirical experience will prove again to be fallible knowledge, and the chances of there being thoughtful life on any planet with liquid surface water are not 100 percent.

If the chances of a planet with thoughtful life are not one in 250 billion stars but rather are, say, one in 10 billion (so that a planet with thoughtful life upon it revolves around one in every 10 billion stars), then there would be twenty-five other such species in our galaxy alone.

Twenty-five thoughtful species in each of 400 billion galaxies equals 10 trillion thoughtful species in the Universe. So I will rename my hypothesis the Misconception of 10 Trillion. I am aware that my knowledge is fallible, and I fully expect my misconception to be wrong by a few trillion in either direction. Nonetheless, 10 trillion, though a very modest number, is sufficient to make the point currently in the crosshairs.

If I Were God

I have set afoot a Universal system that generates species. It's how shit works, Man.

IF I WERE God in a universe of 10 trillion thoughtful species, I'm afraid I would have a hard time caring whether they called me God or Ishtar or Pamela—or indeed, whether they regarded me at all. It's much more likely I would think . . .

"Really, I have heard it all, you know, John. After all, I am God.

"The Hindus are right, just a bit conservative in their guess. I have had 100 quadrillion names. I certainly could not care less whether the Protestants survive the Catholics, much less whether the Flames beat the Canucks. But here is where things get a bit startling for mere persons who, unlike Myself, are not gods. Really, I could not give a damn if any particular thoughtful species survived or not.

"Over eternity I have seen trillions and qua- drillions of such species come and go. Most of them have lasted as long as Human Beings— you know, 200,000 years. Maybe 100 million thoughtful species have gone on to manage their affairs like grown-ups and survived a million years or more. Some of My favorites have even outlasted Earth's dinosaurs, which ran about for a couple of hundred million years...

"I have set afoot a Universal system that generates species. It's how shit works, Man. And, by the way, without disclosing My beliefs about my own existence, please know this for certain: if you think Me smart enough to create a universe in which evolution does not exist, but you think that it is beyond Me to create one in which it does, I'm afraid your opinion of Me is lower than you think it is.

"Look within. There are our diamonds.

"Back over to you, John. Keep up the good work, eh?"

Thanks. You bet, God. Anytime.

How Shit Works, Man

On Earth, the vast variations of species culminated in what we consider to be thoughtful beings. Why should we not expect them to have done so anywhere else? Indeed, why not everywhere else?

IF WE care to, we may understand much better, now, how our Universe works. There are more living species beneath the surface of Earth than there are upon and above it combined. Many of these species are immeasurably ancient and can

exist in conditions that occur on planets anywhere in the Universe. Life persists deep in our frozen, airless rocks and in deep seawater superheated by Earth's core. Indeed, life could do so as easily everywhere in the Universe, even in moons and asteroids or other bits of exploded planets, and in the ice balls of comets.

Whether by chance or intention, life wants to replicate and replenish itself. Where life occurs, DNA tends to persist more in organisms that function better—that is to say, in organisms that replicate more successfully. Gene patterns that replicate more reliably, recur more. Another way of saying it is genes that replicate more reliably tend to survive those that do not. By natural selection and other mechanisms, life tends to exert itself. If life on Earth culminated in plants and eventually animals, why wouldn't we expect life to do so anywhere else, or indeed, everywhere else?

Smarter creatures tend to be more successful competitors; therefore, they tend to replicate more successfully. And so greater varieties of smarter species develop. With ever-greater awareness.

On Earth, the vast variations of species culminated in what we consider to be thoughtful beings. Why should we not expect them to have done so anywhere else? Indeed, why not everywhere else, or at least anywhere there is liquid water?

The Misconception of Zero

Let's be optimists and call that the Misconception of Zero. The chance that we are the most advanced species in the Universe is zero.

SIMPLE ARITHMETIC may show us something another way. Knowing what we know, if among all the stars in the Universe—seven Big Bangs to call the names of each — there occurred once, and once only, an instance of "thoughtful beings," and that happened to be us, that would be a fucking miracle. Granted. But if that were the case, it is all the more a wonder that we don't act like it.

Whatever the number of our equals or better in the Universe might be, to be sure, the odds that we are the most advanced among them are something like one in 10 trillion. We might as well say zero.

"You can say that again."

Let's be optimists and call that the Misconception of Zero. The chance that we are the most advanced species in the Universe is zero.

And so this book's primary misconceptions are

1 The Misconception of 10 Trillion: there are
   at least 10 trillion thoughtful species in the
   Universe; and
2 The Misconception of Zero: the chance that
   we are the most advanced among them is zero.

Even here we would be softly stepping past our
misconception that we already know just about
everything.

What We Don't Know
We Can't Even Add Up

Even all we will learn in the next ninety years is
still the smallest part of all we do not know yet.

THE CURRENT level of our cumulative knowledge on Earth is the result of roughly five
thousand years of learning. Over the majority of
that time, we learned things that we now know
were just wrong. Rome is not the center of the
Universe, the seasons are not the gods' tempers
and the murder of virgin females does not make
crops grow better. Earth is not unique and the sun
does not go around it.

But the vast majority of our knowledge that
is attestable has come to us in the last 250 years,

both the volume of that knowledge and its quality increasing rapidly and at an accelerating rate. So, keeping in mind what we have learned in the ninety years since my mother was born, where the next ninety years will take us is dizzyingly unimaginable. But for certain, even all we will learn in the next ninety years is still the smallest part of all we do not know yet.

Where will another two hundred years of learning take us? What about a thousand more years? Where will a thousand years more learning than ours have taken another thoughtful species? Or many others? What does a million years' learning bring?

If we were wise, we would be humble.

But we seem to be neither.

The Misconceptions and Their Implications

Whether you are an odds guy or not, clearly chances are that most of the things that are knowable in the Universe are already known. Just not by us.

GRANTED, THE Misconception of 10 Trillion and the Misconception of Zero, together, do not *prove* that there is a community of species in this Universe that knows practically everything there is to know. But they do prove that the odds such a community does not exist are so vastly prohibitive as to be reasonably insurmountable.

If we honestly considered the immensity of our present unknown, even if we only considered all that we will learn over the next ninety years, we would be awakened as if from childhood—and two things would become certain.

One, it is obvious that we are dangerously primitive. And two, being a member in good standing of the universal community of thoughtful species is, literally, of unimaginable value.

Whether you are an odds guy or not, clearly chances are that most of the things that are knowable in the Universe are already known. Just not by us. The amount of time that it would take us to learn those things ourselves is beyond calculation. Yet the collective knowledge of the Universe may soon be at our fingertips, if only we could get in touch with those who possess the knowledge, and if only we could demonstrate to them that they needn't fear we would use the knowledge to abuse others the way we now abuse ourselves.

What Knowledge?

Perhaps the Universe is so infinitely abundant that, once you have the knowledge to reach into it, there is no need to bother with being evil.

WHATEVER WONDERS may lie in store, they add up to power and capacity beyond any ever yet dreamt on Earth, even by the Pentagon:

- Computing power that will make what we have now look like rocks in pockets;

- Instantaneous communication across millions of light-years by quantum entanglement and other physics as yet beyond our dreams;

- Practical immortality in the sense of extending our life expectancy to at least a few hundred years. Perhaps awareness will emerge that a few hundred years of abundant prosperity and peace is about all that most individuals need or want; and

- Manipulation of gravity and space-time for travel either way.

We might find that the greatest wonder of all the wonders of the Universe is that knowledge and awareness require power to eradicate evil, that asserting goodness is not merely a choice or a preference but a responsibility and a duty, and that the responsibility is being fulfilled out there, everywhere, now.

With such knowledge would certainly come sufficient power to bring us on Earth to our knees. Why on Earth have we not been invaded? Why is Earth not encrusted with the condos of interstellar bastards, us cleaning their unimaginable asses?

Whoever is keeping the advanced bastards away from Earth, it is not us. But perhaps the Universe is so infinitely abundant that, once you have the knowledge to reach into the stars, there is no need to bother with being evil. Simple Arithmetic does suggest that we have some 10 billion stars per thoughtful species each.

If you were already a member of the community of universal thoughtful species, what sort of being would we look like to *you*? What would you be looking for in newcomers? Why have we not been invited past your velvet rope? Why have we neither seen nor heard from you? If you have a responsibility to stomp evil, why have you not come here to do so? Do you know what ethics are?

The Cumulative Knowledge of the Universe and Its Cost

Learn to pay the fair price of your Liberty and learn to respect your natural bounty. If you do not, you will never meet us. If you do not, who would ever want to meet you?

Dear Earth,

Good day, I am your representative from the Community of Universal Thoughtful Species, and I bring you greetings from Us All. As you are interested in sharing our Cumulative Knowledge, we have a couple of questions to ask you first, questions that would be obvious to any responsible membership manager.

How are you going to get along with 10 trillion other species in our community if you do not respect even your own? If you permit yourselves to treat your own kind so despicably, why would we grant you the power and reach to treat others as badly?

Moreover, if you do not have the highest respect for the natural bounty that has befallen you, if you do not protect and nurture it for all you are worth, why would we afford to you the means to abuse as badly similar treasures elsewhere?

Respect for yourselves and for the natural bounty that has befallen you are minimums of awareness; the absence of either indicates a spirit that we will never permit to be exported into our jurisdiction. When that has happened over the last several hundred million (of your Earth) years, it has always ended badly. We have had eons of experience with species like yours. Our experience overwhelmingly dictates that species of your social maturity must never be permitted anything more than a sophomoric knowledge of astrophysics and cosmology, much less the Cumulative Knowledge of the Community of Universal Thoughtful Species.

Why? Because power combined with selfishness and other childish traits only perpetuates and increases abusiveness. You need only imagine yourself a mother with your fly-bitten infant dying malnourished in your arms while your breasts yield nothing but desert dust. Then take an honest look at your whole world.

However, power combined with compassion opens the door to infinite wealth, of all categories. In this case, unfortunately, examples exist in your world, if at all, only in your future. There may now be some limited, exclusive examples, but that is the point—until they encompass All, they are no example at all. Your Universe is vastly resplendent with such examples of infinite wealth. And if you are smart, you might want to join us and see.

The "concept" that he who gathers owns is about as evolved as the concept of slavery. If this is the height to which you aspire, the Universe will be better off without you.

By behaving in a way that is respectful of ethics, however, you may take the miraculous bounty that has befallen you and make your

Eden. But that requires courage. Because it will not happen unless you Love Your Planet and Handle Your Pricks.

My research informs me that your English word "prick," though ill-mannered by some measure in proper company, is still your most precise and most commonly understood descriptor for persons who are completely selfish, who love to play people to their own advantage and who don't feel the slightest reluctance to break hearts. The importance of my communication with you today is so great that I must risk decorum to ensure precision and common understanding.

And so, yes, "Pricks."

Love your Planet and Handle Your Pricks. Commitment to these two precepts demonstrates appreciation of, and for, what it is that has befallen you. They are minimum prerequisites. Were we to empower you now with our knowledge, we would be empowering the thoughtless selfishness that currently runs wild on Earth. We will not have you out here in the stars taking natural bounty for granted and wreaking your selfish havoc.

Without these prerequisites, it will be lose-lose for all of you. The victims of the injustices will lose, and the perpetrators will always feel insecure and at least vaguely horrified, if only in their sleep. They will not know why they feel this way and will medicate themselves against their feelings with materialism, power and other fleeting, unearned comforts, until all is lost. As an unavoidable consequence, all of you on Earth will be left to stew in your own juices, as have trillions of ignorant species before you, never to learn the lessons that it takes to save and to love your lives, never to learn for reaching your expiry too soon.

The ultimate irony is that most of the lessons that you need to learn, and could have learned but have not, are things that you have already been taught. Yes, we have been watching.

Those lessons may be summarized in one short sentence: Every thoughtful being is entitled to Universal Rights.

They are different from what you call "human rights" in that Universal Rights are accorded to All, whereas you accord your "human rights" only to those in particular countries (and even then, usually not to all). "Human rights" that are only accorded to some, in particular countries are, at best, country club rights. You do not admit all humans into your "free countries," so, for most humans on your Earth, these rights are only available where most humans are not welcome—in your exclusive country clubs.

You have not earned the standing to call them "human rights" until you accord them to all humans.

Universal Rights include

- Respect for and security of the person;
- Food, clothing and shelter;
- Access to the tools of self-improvement, health care, basic capital and justice; and
- A healthy environment.

This basket of rights may be summed up as Freedom. As sure as they are taken for granted by all members of your country clubs, they are a birthright, and thus an entitlement, of Us All, equally, everywhere. Every thoughtful being is entitled to Freedom. These Universal Rights may not be taken for granted until you Handle Your Pricks. Pricks are the only reason Universal Rights are not ubiquitous.

It is not merely our right to accord Universal Rights to All. It is our responsibility.

"Accord," your English transitive verb, is— but is not only—"to bestow"; it is also "to make agree, to make correspond, or to make adapt." Thus, to accord to a person their Universal Rights, it must also be assured that their experience corresponds with their rights. Forgive us if we seem presumptuous, but these are your words. You, not us, have given them their meaning.

As has been heard by many of you since you were children, Rights and Freedom come at a very high cost. "The highest cost," you were told quite earnestly. Those words were truer even than your teachers knew. They thought they meant the cost of giving up their lives fighting for Freedom in wars. It includes that. But it is a price much higher, unfortunately, even than that.

The true cost of Freedom is the responsibility to *accord* that same Freedom, all Universal Rights, to All. All means everybody, notwithstanding the private interests of all Pricks and advantage takers, and all those who act in their service, including ourselves. It is not merely a payment due upon death but comes due again every moment our freedom continues. The dues of Liberty arise daily, and persist throughout our days of Freedom. As beneficiaries of Freedom, we must pay as we go. To earn Freedom, we must strive daily to fulfill the responsibility to accord Freedom to All. It is a simple irony. Liberty never becomes free. Once All are Free, then we all must be kept that way. Free people are responsible for what they know but do not oppose. Liberty is not self-executing.

Only Pricks take and abuse advantage unto themselves. Anyone who is satisfied enjoying their own "freedom," but is careless about what others less fortunate must endure, has not earned Freedom but has merely taken liberties. Prickness is not subjective. It is the failure to pay the true cost of Freedom, the abuse of Universal Rights to our personal advantage, thereby diminishing the Universal Rights of others without their consent. This diminishment of others' rights is what distinguishes hoarding Pricks from those merely making good money.

The epithet is well merited not only by those who take advantage but also by all those who either share in the advantage taken or act in the service of advantage takers. You may not be a heartless perpetrator yourself, but you may still take much delight in the dividends heartless perpetrators pay. This is but one of the mechanisms whereby Prickness extends to its shareholders, employees and customers.

Although most of your country club members do not, themselves, procure slaves, abuse workers or poison environments, they engage in economic activity that benefits from those behaviors. Ninety percent of the leather worn in your shoes, belts and jackets, or used for handbags and wallets to carry your money, was tanned in South Asia, where people, who are the same as any of us, work submerged above their breasts in tanning fluids that have been banned elsewhere on Earth for forty years. They stir the hides in the tanning chemicals with their legs and soft heels because sticks and paddles are too rough on the delicate leathers. Similar travesty yields gold, diamonds, chocolate, most hydrocarbons, chemicals, rare earths, minerals, manufactured goods and much else from your "developing world."

Universal Rights are crushed under the necessity of your cheap and convenient energy, leather coats and shoes, jewelry, electronic devices, tires, runway fashions and runaway jet fuel. It is no wonder that, although you may care about slavery, you do not notice this so much. It is easy to be seduced and confused by advantage.

Every person is entitled to Universal Rights. America and Earth's other constitutional democracies have come very close to understanding rights. They fall short only in extent and in scope. As free people, it is our responsibility to accord these Universal Rights to All. Very often, our only way is against the whingeing and griping of Pricks. But nevertheless, to act is not merely our choice, nor is it just a preference. It is our duty as free persons.

The natural bounty that has befallen you Earthlings is not merely an astonishingly beautiful planet but also one that functions so magnificently well as to give rise to you and to provide sustenance for you and for all of your descendants. You only deserve it if you conserve it. But your descendants deserve it even if you do not. The responsibility is inescapable. Only behavior is optional.

The chances of having both such a planet and consciousness, as Earthlings do, may be one in 10 billion stars. Those odds are miraculous. Permitting Pricks to lay to waste Earth's miraculous eternal capacity in the service of their own selfishness at the expense of the birthright of yourselves and your descendants is a gross abrogation of one's responsibility to their place, to their kind and to their kindness.

Now you see.

You may allow your tiny planet and all who are upon it to go to hell; we in the Community of Universal Thoughtful Species will neither save you nor stop you. But we have timeless experience that requires us to ensure that your kind, who have not learned these first lessons of respect and responsibility, never be permitted to reach the stars.

Rest assured that we live up to our responsibilities. There *are* none like you out here. We have handled all of our Pricks, and we ensure that Universal Rights are accorded to All eternally.

As the wise among you will realize, the very phenomenon that you are not already overrun by alien Pricks is proof of the fact. Ask why there has been no radio contact and you may as well ask why there have been no smoke signals or jam-can-on-a-string telephone calls. The reason you have not heard from us before now is not because we couldn't. And it's not because communication is limited by the speed of light. That limitation depends on an understanding of physics that is new to you in your mother's lifetime. To your present understanding, "radio waves"— light—are as fast as you've got. Yet quantum entanglement, what your Einstein called "*spukhafte Fernwirkung*," or "spooky action at a distance," seemed to have instantaneous effect across unlimited space over no time at all, absolutely in the same moment. In the next hundred years, you will learn as much as you did in the last five thousand. I think it still may be a bit early for you to declare there is no means in the physical universe except radio waves to communicate across vast space. It's like your Homer Simpson saying Rolls-Royce is the Cadillac of cars.

The reason you haven't heard from us is, until you embrace awareness, we couldn't be bothered—the same reason you don't call your annoying acquaintance who only gets in touch when they want your money.

Learn to pay the fair costs of your Liberty, and learn to respect your natural bounty. If you do not, you will never meet us. If you do not, who would ever want to meet you?

Or, of course, if you choose, you may live in peace and bounty practically forever. Would you like to go out?

With all due respect, you only get this Letter once.

Sincere best wishes,

Your CUTS rep

Meanwhile, Back Here on Earth

ALL RIGHT. Well. Thanks very much. That is what I would have said if I were a CUTS rep. It's a lot to take in, and there is obviously a lot more to come. With all of your experience, you just know that it will be no time at all until we hear the whingeing of Pricks:

"Yeah, right. How could we possibly accomplish all that that implies? Good luck with that! Responsibility for all, the world over? Pah! What about *our* freedoms?"

"What about our private property rights? What's mine is mine, right?"

"And what about sovereignty? We've got a deal here. We do things our way; Saudi does things theirs. End of story."

"Science works good enough for us the way it is. If it ain't broke, don't fix it."

"You're just one of those fainthearted, commie, one-worldie radicals. I think I smell a redistributionist. If that's what you call an idea, you're right, we have limited interest. Next."

"Who the hell are we to say what's right for everybody? Who does this guy think he is? Christ Almighty."

"We've had it up to here with these bleeding-heart socialist liberals who say they want to save everybody because it's politically correct."

Yes, Pricks, indeed. You have had it up to here, and still there is so much further up to go. It is a lot to take in and it doesn't make it easier to hear while ears are jangling with the clangorous echo of losing advantage.

Don't forget, you did ask.

3

The Terms of Interference

And it is none of our business. Right?

WHEN WE WERE kids, we thrilled as the
Lone Ranger, one of the greatest humans
ever, chased bad guys (Mexicans), spurring to the
galloping rhythm: *tadadum tadadum tada dump
dump dump*. The hombres raced for the border
to the same pounding measure. Get across the
Rio Grande, then you're scot-free. The banditos
would celebrate by flipping the bird, knowing
Kemosabe would never cross after them. Scoundrels on the other side of the river were somehow
different and need not fear the Lone Ranger
coming across to even the score. Across that line,
victims must look out for, and perpetrators may
serve, themselves.

Why? Well, jurisdiction of course, Sovereignty, the basket of "rights" continually insisted upon by those in power for thousands of years. At one time, only kings (and their friends) enjoyed this divine right of Sovereignty. Now whole countries do, around two hundred of them. Thus, in one nation it is declared, "Thou shalt not cut off the clitorises of young women," while in another, with nothing more than a "Sorry, quite Sovereign, you know," they gash, horrifyingly, away. And it's none of our business. Right?

If that is right, there is something terribly unsatisfying about that righteousness, particularly for the victims. Kemosabe no cross Rio Grande? Perhaps shame on Kemosabe. Heap big shame. No cross Rio Grande to chase Pricks but only to import strawberries, *limons*, brussels sprouts and tequila all winter. Only cross Rio Grande for vacations. Not for responsibility.

Sticking Our Nose into the Unruly Behavior of Scoundrels

That we have the responsibility is evident to every kid in second grade.

WHY MAY young women who are raped, mutilated, murdered and discarded in the dumps of Ciudad Juárez not expect to be protected from rapists, mutilators and murderers, at least as much as are the women of El Paso, across the Rio Grande, in Texas, USA? (Please permit me to recommend Roberto Bolaño's 2666, his monumental account of the crime of the century, in which thousands of young women have been raped, mutiated and murdered, and not a single case solved. This unspeakable barbarism, possibly a sport, continues as of this writing, in late 2016.) Or what about the captive sex slaves of ISIS and Boko Haram?

When we dwindle to excuses like Sovereignty or Religion in the defense of child genital mutilation, rape and murder, everyone knows the score. Perpetrators know they will not be stopped, and both victims and bystanders quite properly feel disgusted. But why must we feel helpless? Why, at some line in the sand, does evil become none of our business?

If we were to shoulder the responsibility and chase down relentless, interminable, insufferable Pricks, disregarding their "defenses," like Sovereignty, Religion or private property, upon what authority could we ride across the Rio Grande and run them down on "their" turf? That we have the responsibility is evident to every kid in second grade (though everything changes outside the school grounds).

How do we justify sticking our nose into the unruly behavior of sovereign, religious or other Pricks who defile the rights of others just because they can?

Ironically, the proper authority may arise from the same body of common law upon which we all insist—Pricks and all the rest of us country clubbers alike—to protect our property rights in domestic and commercial transactions: the Law of Trusts. Although what follows is a bit suit *and* tie, I encourage you to trundle onward for a bit, which I grant will bring you wandering perilously close to legalese, though still, it may be just the fix for our ticket.

Trusts

Trusts prevent cheating in relationships that naturally give rise to an extraordinary opportunity to abuse something that belongs to another.

WHEN YOU pay money into a lawyer's office, your check is made out to the lawyer "in Trust." You have created a legal relationship, a legal entity, called a Trust. When lawyers take money "in Trust," the law makes them trustee of that money and makes you the client beneficiary of the Trust. The obligation that the law imposes upon trustees is called a "fiduciary obligation." It is the highest obligation imposed by civil law, and it requires the trustee to act in the absolute utmost good faith.

Trusts are a strange entity, originally created by common law, then adopted by legislation. Their essential purpose is to prevent cheating in relationships that naturally give rise to an extraordinary opportunity to abuse something that belongs to another. The Trust arises at law precisely because such circumstances provide—to the lawyers, for example—just such an extraordinary opportunity for abuse. They might take your money and use it on the stock market, at the racetrack or in a cocaine deal, and as long as it is returned to you when required, you are none the wiser. But your money was put at risk, which you did not authorize, and that is a breach of the Trust. If they spend your money on one pack of cigarettes—even if they replace the money—that is a breach of the Trust.

No matter what happens, without exception, the trustee is liable to the beneficiary *to not abuse the extraordinary opportunity* that comes of holding the money.

If the beneficiary's money is used or risked in any way, except in strict accordance with instructions and all of the trustee's other obligations at

law, the trustee is personally liable to the beneficiary for all losses. So complete is the duty
owed that, should your money be "lost" by your
trustee, all of the trustee's assets, whether real
estate or personal property, will go to repay you.
This includes their cottage, their boat, their
watch, their rare dog, and gifts to their spouse,
family and friends. Everything.

Property is the simplest but not the only
case of the law following the concepts of Trusts.
Since the founding of their country, America's
courts have been advancing case law brought
on the Public Trust Doctrine, a part of American
jurisprudence that provides that government
holds essential natural resources, including
navigable water and the atmosphere, "in Trust"
for present and future generations. It is said to
be a breach of the Public Trust to take secret
profit (bribes) for the administration of authority
entrusted to public office.

By legislation, corporate directors owe a fiduciary obligation to their corporation. All agents
are fiduciaries to their principles. So if a real
estate agent makes a side deal on your transac-
tion and takes more money out of the deal than
the contract commission, they breach the Trust
and the obligation.

Although the First Amendment may protect
the right to lie in America (see page 87), trustees

do not enjoy the protection of that dubious excuse. When trustees breach a fiduciary duty, they do not get to say, "It's a free country."

The conditions of the trust and fiduciary obligation are set by the evidence in the circumstances, but when the evidence is unclear or in dispute, the court *always* goes against the trustee. A trustee can never win at "he said, she said."

Without these fiduciary obligations, there would be innumerable untrustworthy lawyers and accountants, and estate planning would be severely limited. Business the world over would come to a chaotic standstill, and there would be many, many more successful scoundrels. Lawyers would be almost impossible to control without the Law of Trusts. Most of their professional fees arise in part by the execution by them of Trusts, the Trusts that protect your funds in their hands. Where these trusts do not prevail, bribery is everything.

Our capacity to develop economically depends on property owners (real estate and all other property, including cash) being confident in their right of ownership, to own what they own, securely. Trusts provide that assurance in the law's highest degree.

"What does this have to do with Universal Rights?"

The Law of Trusts provides a remarkable tool for enforcement of rights in court. Its evolution depends on the creativity of lawyers to help the court understand and recognize the emerging trusts.

"Upon what Trusts might Universal Rights and the accordance of them to all others depend?"

In a constitutional democracy that proclaims life, liberty and the pursuit of happiness the cornerstones of their constitutional accord, Universal Rights must be a component of the Public Trust.

If accordance of Universal Rights is our duty, what sense would that duty make without a legal mechanism to enforce it? Upon what basis will we justify enforcement against someone who proclaims, for example, religious freedom, or protection of a sovereign boundary, when she insists upon slashing off the clitoris of her twelve-year-old niece with an otherwise useless old rusty tin-can top?

What are the proper terms for interference, for sticking our noses into the unruly privacy of sovereign or religious Pricks?

Those who have made it this far in these, my tidings, will have detected the influx of a drier note. That is about to continue, but only for a bit. Although I am in recovery from having myself been a lawyer, still, their language, well handled, is the best for some things. And so, for those who might plow on, I hope color commentary will entice you further where mere light may not. I'll warrant that when this is threshed and ruminated, there will be all the time in the world for mixed metaphors. Some of what follows, I did not make up.

The Principles that Vindicate Intervention

And who am I to propose them?

"WHO ARE you to say…?"

I know a thing or two about the wealthy and about Pricks. I have been both. I've met ridiculously wealthy guys, and having been one of them too, they don't fool me much. I owned a quarter of a company that went public and achieved market capitalization of almost $2 billion. At one time, I nearly bumped Keanu Reeves off the list of top 100 richest Canadians at just under $300 million. Now, I'm mostly over that.

I'm a lawyer who escaped the day-to-day practice of law years ago, but I practiced for fifteen years and acted as trustee in thousands of transactions. I have been charged with felonies in the United States, convicted and sentenced to prison, and I was party to a US$250 million forfeiture for transferring online gambling money. So I have been treated to the brutal disdain and disrespect that comes of being Uncle Sam's prisoner in these times.

My most important credential is that there are those to whom I, too, have been a Prick. Millions of them. For starters, I have been an importer of leather from India. And owner of a private jet burning more fuel than if I drove everywhere in three loaded semis.

But the situation for most Pricks is complicated, and not everything we Pricks do is Prickish. For years, I have been a director on behalf of the preeminent ecologist David Suzuki. And I am a co-founder of DeSmogBlog group, a chain of leading blogs about climate and the PR pollution that clouds climate science. So perhaps what follows will also help me atone.

I offer the following principles to vindicate our intervention on behalf of the victims of Pricks everywhere.

4

The Higher Trusts

*Extraordinary influence comes
with an inevitable extraordinary
opportunity for abuse.*

EVERYONE IS entitled to Universal Rights and Freedom. The essential attribute of Freedom is to not have to give up entitlement without consent.

An implied Trust is breached every time Pricks rig shit to their own personal advantage, thereby abusing extraordinary influence against the Universal Rights of others.

There are three situations in our society to which extraordinary influence, power and advantage automatically appertain. Wealth, Public Authority and Public Information each give rise to a level of influence that is unmatched in persons who do not possess any of those attributes. That they come with such extraordinary influence is evident to every kid in second grade. (The author hereafter will rely upon this reference so frequently that, at times, it will be signified by "ibid." The less mannered might say it suggests "duh.")

This extraordinary influence comes with an inevitable *extraordinary opportunity for abuse*. So it must come together with the corresponding responsibility that it never be abused by the entrusted individual for their personal benefit where their advantage taken diminishes the Universal Rights of any other person without that other's consent.

Wealth

As is aptly demonstrated by their prosperity, Freedom has worked especially well for the wealthy, and the good among them will be delighted to pay the true costs of that Freedom.

THERE IS an obvious power that exudes from Wealth, and in degree it bears direct proportion. In exactly the same way most rockers don't discuss tinnitus, most wealthy do not admit to the advantages that come with their affluence. These include extraordinary access to and influence over politicians, and the ability to gang up and then accumulate and hoard wealth at will, by, for instance, getting the jump on market profit opportunities that are not available to those without immediate financing. I find very apt a turn of phrase fashioned by Adam Smith, the philosopher who introduced the concept of the invisible hand. Although it is "a matter of fact too obvious to require any instances to prove it," most wealthy people and five-ninths of the US Supreme Court (as evidenced by Citizens United, a 2010 case that eradicated major limits on election campaign spending) are in denial that any such power comes with wealth.

Although a majority of wealthy people may deny their extraordinary power, a minority abuse it, constantly and for all it's worth. Whether they poison land or water, or simply ignore and abuse the hundreds of millions who are sick and dying in squalor, their wealth has been taken from all others who remain diminished by abuse of the obvious power of the wealthy to take advantage unto themselves. Trumpeting their "freedom" that has been protected for them by us all, they take wealth for themselves, disregarding the true cost of Freedom, the responsibility to accord that same Freedom to all others.

Wealth implies the extraordinary power to unfairly impose upon or diminish the Universal

Rights of others, and sometimes all others, on Earth. Wealth comes from Earth, and most often it is by the toil of, or in selling necessaries to, working people. Wealth is accumulated within the security of the institutions of government that the people provide and maintain with their taxes for the benefit of us all.

People assure Freedom to pursue wealth, entrusting that it be pursued responsibly. Therefore, the extraordinary power of Wealth must be exercised only in the utmost good faith—that is, in Trust. The abuse of that Trust to the diminishment of the Universal Rights of any others is a breach of the Trust and of fiduciary duty.

Wealth is not a problem; it is miraculous. But it comes in Trust. One of the first duties of all Wealth must be to provide in fair portion for the accordance of Universal Rights to us all. Good Wealth pays its fair share to fulfill the Responsibilities of Freedom. Any who selfishly hoard in disregard of this responsibility are in breach of this fiduciary duty. These would be Pricks. For those seeking further information, *Dark Money* by Jane Mayer is a very good start.

As is aptly demonstrated by their prosperity, Freedom has worked especially well for the wealthy, and the good among them will be delighted to pay their true cost of that Freedom.

But it is our responsibility to require that the same fair share be paid by them all.

Wealth not only may, it must, pay its share in direct proportion, no more than that but not a bit less, to fully accord, restore and maintain Universal Rights for All.

Public Authority

That these breaches of the Trust usually correspond with officials receiving political support and contribution is, again, "a matter of fact too obvious to require any instances to prove it."

EVERYBODY KNOWS that Wealth isn't the only way things get rigged. Even more obvious power is entrusted to those appointed to government authority, the authority we struggled so mightily to wrest from kings at no small cost, and that we lend back to our government only upon the strictest conditions.

Authority is granted by people to government to be exercised for the benefit of all citizens, of all of their descendants and of all of the commons. Among authority's highest duties must be the duty to accord and maintain Universal Rights.

Public Authority provides extraordinary power and influence, and it, too, includes the power to abuse that authority for personal advancement, or for the benefit of separate classes of persons, without regard for the interests of others. (Ibid.) We need only look at the pollution of the Athabasca tar sands tailings ponds or the atrocities committed under Syrian president Bashar al-Assad. Therefore, Public Authority comes to one in Trust and must be exercised only in the utmost good faith. This duty falls upon all public officials, all officials appointed by them and anybody else who is entrusted with the execution of Public Authority.

Abuse of the Power of Public Authority is a breach of Trust and is thus a breach of fiduciary duty. Common examples include preferring certain industries regardless of their true costs to public health (guns), environment (fossil fuels) or fiscal security (banking deregulation). That these breaches of Trust usually correspond with officials receiving political support and contribution (see Wealth on page 60) is, again, "a matter of fact too obvious to require any instances to prove it." (Ibid.)

The majority in government probably deny abuse of their power, though they, too, very likely act in the service of its abusers. A minority absolutely abuses it on behalf of particular interests that do not necessarily accord with, and may go against, the Universal Rights of all people, their descendants and the commons. Most unfortunately, these are more Pricks. Once again, *Dark Money* is offered as primer. I was most interested to see the involvement of United States Supreme Court Justice Antonin Scalia in this cabal.

Universal Rights diminished by abuse of Public Authority must be restored and the abusers made to account for their breach of the fiduciary duty.

Public Information

Because democracy is utterly dependent upon an accurately informed electorate, intentionally messing with Public Information is subversive of democracy.

"I read the news today, oh boy."

Democracy, to function successfully, requires a properly informed electorate. It requires reliable information about both government policy and any private behavior in which public regulation has an interest. The public must know what goes on so that they may form opinions about whether proper regulation is being observed. Therein lies another extraordinary opportunity for abuse of influence—the avoidance of proper scrutiny by the manipulation of public awareness.

Public Information provides an extraordinary opportunity for abuse because the less selective in the audience are putty in the hands of those in power. The discerning and inquisitive find their own advice, though they might be wary—as is often misattributed to Mark Twain, "if you don't read the newspaper, you're uninformed. If you do read the newspaper you're misinformed." Still, today reliable information (as well as every other kind) is pretty much at our fingertips, if only fingertips knew where to click. And where not.

Unfortunately, huge swaths of the audience are not discerning but are ready vessels, wide open to persuasive suggestion, whether by domestic industrial titans or Vladimir Putin. These people embrace information not on the basis of its accuracy and reliability but merely because it is what's in "the news." For example, Fox News network declares President Obama is a Muslim with no legitimate birth certificate, oil and gas corporation ExxonMobil cares deeply about climate change, and everything is "fair and balanced." Social media is swamped with these mis-directions. (Ibid.) Just check your Facebook feed to read about chem-trails, the anti-vaxx movement and the conspiracy theory

that human-caused climate change is a fraud
by Chinese like David Suzuki to obtain hundreds
of billions in university grants.

People are swayed en masse by the information that is dished up to them by "networks."
Some networks are careless about what they say,
claiming, "We are only reporting the news."

Within other networks, stories are cooked
up that spin sympathetically with the private or
political interests that they represent. The power
of public information is actively manipulated to
whittle and hew public knowledge and thus train
public awareness. Communications professionals are commercially and professionally obliged
to promote the interests of their clients, whether
private parties or political movements, whose
private interests do not necessarily coincide with
those of the electorate or of the commons.

But there are other responsibilities that trump
the private, the professional and the commercial.
Because democracy is utterly dependent upon
an accurately informed electorate, intentionally
messing with Public Information is subversive of
democracy. It need not be repeated to what class
such subversives relegate themselves. (Ibid.)
Public Information professionals—including
politicians, educators, clerics and "the media"—
take every opportunity to say whatever they

want, whether it is verified, balanced, completely frank or completely the contrary.

Politicians and Privateers are held accountable for their misleading spin about as often as cell phones crash airliners. Abusers take that opportunity incessantly, self-servingly, and excuse misinformation as free speech:

"There is no connection between tobacco and lung disease."

"There is no proven scientific relationship between burning fossil fuels and climate change."

"Clean coal is better for the environment than wind generators, and it doesn't matter anyway because carbon capture technology is really taking off."

They need prove nothing because, as Jim Hoggan points out in *Climate Cover-Up*, it is sufficient to their selfish purposes merely to raise doubt.

Public Information professionals are trusted by the public to provide facts and opinions. They know, and intend, that their facts and opinions will be relied upon as having been provided in good faith. This includes the opportunity to spin the entrusted information. The extraordinary Power and Influence of Public Information must not be abused for personal advancement, or for the benefit of exclusive persons or groups disregarding the common obligation of free people to the Universal Rights of All. The influence must be exercised only in the utmost good faith. Confounding public awareness by misinformation is abuse of the Influence of Public Information; it is a breach of Trust and thus, a breach of fiduciary duty.

Journalism is our most important institution for holding to account both private and public officials. The people's primary tools for keeping officials responsible must not be turned against the people, subverting their democracy by perverting their information. This perversion must never be excused by such misbegotten claims as free speech.

The cult that perverts free speech to protect deceit must be cured of its bloat and made to accord with the Responsibilities of Freedom and with Universal Rights.

A World You Can Trust

The costs of complete world development certainly could not exceed the current costs of world military. Unfortunately, it will take the genius of another generation to realize that the best defense is placing Goodness on the offense.

WEALTH, PUBLIC Authority and Public Information are entrusted knowing that tremendous, extraordinary influence inevitably comes with each. They exist in our culture because the people create them. People create Wealth by their labors and other economic activity. People lend authority to government. And people entrust the Public Information they require to professionals, each of whom must assume the coinciding obligation: utmost good faith.

What people have created and have given up in Trust must not be accepted by the trustees except on the condition that all Universal Rights and the Responsibilities of Freedom are completely respected. Acceptance of the benefits, whether of Freedom or of a Higher Trust, but not their proper coincidental responsibilities, defines the Prick. The Trusts imply a right and, moreover, a responsibility to put an end to all such abuse of advantage. Here we might look at ourselves.

The Highest Trust is Freedom. Freedom is the basket that holds all the other Trusts. It is the unique situation in our world by which extraordinary influence, power and advantage automatically appertain to an entire society. Those of us who enjoy it possess an invincible power to hold unto ourselves the advantages of Freedom. We are deep over our heads in these advantages, so deep that we must stockpile our wealth in huge vaults beneath mountains, while in Darfur dusty breasts on skeletons with skin yield only dying whimpers.

All of us who have the benefits of Freedom are Freedom's trustees. We must discharge our duty to pay Freedom's true cost by ensuring it for all others as for ourselves. With only the utmost good faith.

If any of us is entitled to Universal Rights and Freedom, then we All are. Longstanding common law on the Public Trust Doctrine provides that government holds essential natural resources in Trust for the people. It ought to be our guide in the emergence of Freedom and Universal Rights being recognized as resources so essential to constitutional democracy that they too must be administered as Public Trust.

If these Rights and Responsibilities are admitted, then there follow certain consequences. Among the consequences will be the conspicuously many objectors, their selfish objections to be met, their contrived obstacles to be overcome.

In the same way that our responsibility to properly care for our children is not diminished by our uncertainty at times about how best to provide that care, our responsibility to All others to act on behalf of all victims of Pricks is not abated by not knowing yet, in any particular case, how to proceed.

But is it fair to have a duty imposed upon us that we have no idea how to discharge? It is said that philosopher Immanuel Kant thought, "ought implies can," and, therefore, "cannot" implies "has no duty to." If Kant is right, then I must be wrong and we can't have a duty that seems impossible to perform.

Whether that is what Kant meant, I can't say. But it seems clear to me that even when we don't know our way, once it seems quite likely that we have a duty, we must find our way.

Neither are our responsibilities diminished by our failure to have acted upon them (honestly) in the past. Having been wrong does not require that we continue to be wrong merely to be consistent. That we have unjustly forced our culture upon others in the past cannot exonerate us from properly according Universal Rights now and onward.

Obstacles and objections will probably be endless. However, I expect that, as well, proper claims will come forward that are undeniable, and will be carried forward until they too are taken for granted.

It is now wonderfully common in many places that homosexuals are entitled to the same respect as everyone else, no matter whom they may love. When my mom was born, it was a different story. But did my mom have a duty to stick up for Oscar Wilde? Or Truman Capote? Was she morally excused, or even forbidden, from sticking up for them because so many others at the time thought *they* were? Is duty a matter of common opinion blowing in the winds of popularity? Are rights?

For a current example of another commonly accepted crime against which we might invoke Universal Rights, let us consider the protection of young women from having their clitorises sliced away. When that young woman shows up at our border, we must let her in *or* follow her back home to put our foot down on her behalf. If any person is in physical danger sufficiently to establish refugee status, these young women must be. Soon these women will learn that they have a choice, and they will find out to whom near them they may turn for help. We will have demonstrated that justice is available to those who demand it, and that we may be relied upon to ensure that the right is accorded. Within a generation, we will have gone from indulging in cruel oblivion to seeing physical security for all adolescent girls become wonderfully common, too.

Then, as we ensure the security of adolescent female persons, we will learn the proper terms of our responsible interference on behalf of all victims of Pricks. From that experience, we will encounter a full range of obstacles. And we will learn what to do with them. We will learn the limits of Sovereignty, of Religion, of Wealth and of Authority, and as well, we will determine the proper extent for the use of sufficient force notwithstanding any self-serving objections. After that we need only go the rest of the way.

The costs of establishing such development may seem high. If we thought selling fossil fuels for profit faced an inconvenient truth in climate science, then it will be easy to imagine inconvenience in fulfilling the Higher Trusts. But the security and productivity that will be developed over the years by the recognition of the Higher Trusts will cultivate wealth enough to dwarf any that could ever be hoarded.

Hoarding is the wet dream of economic accomplishment. It is illusory wealth because it comes without the goodwill of its creators and thus always comes with the anxiety of its loss. Good money is not hoarded. It is earned, but only after it pays its fair share for both the preservation of Universal Rights and the proper costs of the institutions that protect Freedom for us all, then may good money be saved. It is within the framework of those institutions we support with our taxes that Wealth was produced and accumulated. Once Wealth has paid its fair share in support of those institutions, then good money may be accumulated endlessly by any to whom the hobby appeals.

The costs of complete world development certainly could not exceed the current costs of world military. Unfortunately, it will take the genius of another generation to realize that the best defense is placing Goodness on the offense.

If sharing is imagined to be too expensive, watch carefully the true costs of not sharing as they unfold horrifyingly around us. Go holiday in the slums of Dhaka, of Jakarta or of Mumbai.

But if we live up to our duties as the beneficiaries of Freedom, when all upon Earth are well cared for, mission ready and pulling heartily on oars, wealth will profuse forth. I think economists call it productivity. We will have fulfilled the democratic ideal, demonstrating the highest faith in ordinary people to be great when provided with the opportunity, when they know the game is not rigged against them. Anything else is very likely advantage abuse and hoarding.

We may "imagine no possessions," as John Lennon proposed, and we should. But I do not recommend it as a policy at this time. Rather, for now, I recommend sharing. That is, being responsible with Freedom and with Universal Rights. Pricks, who have profited by taking liberties unpaid for, and by disregarding Universal Rights, will relinquish the full portion of their ill-gotten wealth to the commons, and we All will become their successor stakeholders, for Good. That will have been an excellent day at the office.

Of the many obstacles in our society that deter us from exercising our responsibilities to all others, and so shelter both Pricks and their misbehavior, there are two important examples that ought to be considered closely. Corporations, and the limits to their obligations, are one. The other is sovereignty. A closer look at both of these phenomena may chasten two such stupefying obstacles.

5

Nonhuman Legal Persons and the Minimum of Human Decency

Not only may corporations behave poorly, they must.

WHEN ADAM SMITH presented his thoughts about the coincidental benefits of pursuing self-interest in *The Wealth of Nations* in 1776, he had already written what *he* thought to be his superior work, *The Theory of Moral Sentiments*, in 1759. Smith advocated for the pursuit of self-interest, but he also thought that people (quaintly, he called people "men") were naturally "good," and that they had "sympathy," which led them to take an interest in the well-being of others. His "invisible hand" is first seen in the earlier work, doing good in natural sympathy for others less fortunate, whether or not the prosperous consciously recognized or intended it.

He thought, quite correctly, that the good ones of us will be fair, and even more, he thought we would be generous. He also thought there would be enough good ones among us that they would naturally make up for any others. Today, the evidence for this last bit is less convincing. However, little did Smith know that, eventually, the law would grant to corporations the status of legal persons but spare them the responsibilities of being good ones.

Legal person status for corporations evolved in common law through the nineteenth century based on the idea that people, who have constitutional protection against arbitrary government interference, ought to have no less protection when they act collectively in an enterprise. Corporations were granted the status of legal persons to protect people who act collectively in enterprise from arbitrary authority. So corporations could now enter into contracts, buy and sell, sue and be sued. And pay tax. They became legal persons long before women did, and *that* was long before blacks or indigenous peoples were awarded status as "persons" under the law.

Although corporations now enjoy legal personhood, they do not have all of the attributes of natural legal persons (humans). Corporations do not vote and they may not claim Fifth Amendment protection against self-incrimination. Quite obviously, they do not get sick, starve, die, fall in love or lose children.

Corporations are a powerful tool to create goods, technology and services on a vast scale. They employ huge numbers in their service. And they provide the mechanism to generate vast amounts of revenue, creating for very large groups more wealth than has ever existed on Earth. Of all the things we will need to fulfill our responsibilities as the beneficiaries of Freedom here on Earth, wealth is certainly very high on the list.

But before this can be mistaken as an apologia for the running-dog capitalist corporations of unbridled self-interest, in spite of all the good done by corporations, they are also the instruments of horrifying irresponsibility the world over. Still, most of it is not their fault.

Corporations are a different sort of legal person, one that must follow all the rules that they are forced by law to follow, but no others. They need not—indeed, must not—follow any rules that they are *not* required to follow by law—for example, moral rules—if it would be at the expense of their shareholders. So if no rules are enforced, then corporate directors would be in breach of their duty were they to waste their shareholders' money voluntarily cleaning up the Athabasca tar sands tailings ponds, a residue of their profits unprecedented in history.

Not only *may* corporations behave poorly, they must. Corporations don't do ethics; they only do law, and they do the absolute minimum of that. It may seem an unfair thing to say, but I am sure it is not. Corporations are a bit like guns. Everything depends upon how they are regulated. And whose finger's on the trigger.

"Unless the law says a chemical is harmful, it is not. And we will peddle it or dump it as long as we like until we're forced by law to stop."

Like Balcorp, the Canadian asbestos company sanctioned by former prime minister Stephen Harper, despite knowing what we all know, to peddle Canadian asbestos to India. Or like Exxon. When it comes to selling hazardous materials or dumping resource extraction's toxic spawn, the law makes it your responsibility, nonhuman corporate legal person, to be a dick.

"Clean up your mess."

"Yeah? Make me."

We created corporations and endowed them with all of the legal rights but sadly few of the obligations of being a proper person. These nonhuman legal persons have a duty to disregard *all* negative side effects, whether mischief or havoc, that authority does not actively force them to avoid.

Now we encourage them to produce, on our behalf, not only horror for millions in Sudan, Nigeria, Somalia and throughout the "Third World," but also deprivation both physical and emotional for hundreds of millions more of the merely poor, much closer to and even within our country clubs, and across Earth in vast cities.

We actively encourage them because we do not regulate them. Talisman Energy, an Alberta company, took hundreds of millions in profits generated in very large part upon the deprivation in Darfur. Royal Dutch Shell's Nigerian production dumps oil and toxic waste, and makes billions, on the backs of Nigerians deprived of basic protections by the corrupt Pricks who run the country and loot its resources for their personal profit. Shell and Talisman go anywhere they may do, without regulation, what would never be permitted here at home in the country clubs. We would regulate such behavior here, and they would never expect we would not. We should regulate our companies away too, but instead, we take dividends. Still, we can't blame corporations for doing what we refuse to prohibit.

At one time, like Smith, we thought good people would look after the less fortunate, but now, most of the wealth on Earth is held by these nonhuman legal persons, whose duty it is to not share. Their duty is to exploit every not-illegal avenue to accumulate and hoard on behalf of private interests. Corporations do not measure civil wrongs such as pollution, misrepresentation and regulatory breaches on a moral scale, but only on the scales of economy, having regard for nothing but the financial costs, the amount of court-ordered damages or fines, and legal fees. If you can settle for damages or pay a penalty and still make money, fine. No corporation has ever gone to jail. Curiously, their human functionaries rarely do either—though there have been cases (ahem).

Eventually, corporations have found themselves in the position that it doesn't matter what they say or do, nobody will hold feet to the fire, excepting only small cash fines. It has quickly become evident that a board of directors would be irresponsible in its duty to shareholders' interests if they did any more than only the absolute minimum required by human decency, because the business advantage comes at no greater cost than a bit of cash. Or even better, toxic dumping in the tar sands tailings ponds—free, excepting only the cost to Albertans for hundreds of years to come.

"We did everything the regulators made us do," say Suncor, Syncrude, Shell and all the other tar sands oil companies.

Smith did not foresee most of the money in the world belonging to these nonhuman legal persons. Nor could he foresee the effect such permissiveness for corporations would have upon human behavior.

Worse than Real Persons— But, Hey, Wait a Minute

Why shouldn't individuals, as well, have the right to do the absolute minimum cried out for by humanity?

IN TIME, we discovered that, "in business," we human legal persons were at an unfair disadvantage when competing with nonhuman legal persons (corporations), because of burdensome morals and human decency. Why shouldn't individuals, as well, have the right to do the absolute minimum cried out for by humanity? As human moral agents in business, why should we suffer a higher duty when it comes to the plainly wrong behavior that we condone in corporations? Who could blame individuals for claiming that they, too, ought to have the equal right to behave badly? Corporations were made legal persons so that individuals who conduct enterprise as a collective would be protected by law and not be put at a disadvantage.

"We did not make corporations legal persons *to put ourselves at a disadvantage*. It shouldn't be 'better' to be incorporated. Fair's fair, right?"

Tacitly, we agreed. In business, we individuals may behave the same way as nonhuman legal persons. Where good persons would never have thought to step, now we trample blindly, chanting our mantra, "That's business." We all know, now, that when someone says, "That's business," somebody else just got fucked. Now we have individual business people entitled to, and corporations required to, act with the absolute minimum of discretionary human decency.

There is a vast area of human activity and judgment where, though we may not be prohibited from a particular behavior by law, we might not do it anyway because it seems unfair, hurtful, harmful or just wrong and everybody knows it. It is not illegal to lie to your partner. Call it discretionary decency. There is an unpopular branch of philosophy entirely devoted to the topic, called Ethics. Call me old-fashioned.

Lying is a good example. Lying is wrong, right?

The First Amendment, which protects the right to free speech, also protects a right to lie. In 2012, the US Supreme Court threw out a case (United States v. Alvarez) against a fellow who lied about having been in the military. He was charged under the Stolen Valor Act, legislation by the US Congress that prohibits claiming you had served in the military when you had not. But the Stolen Valor Act was struck down by the Supreme Court deciding even those lies are constitutionally protected free speech.

I may not know much, but this much I do know. If you can lie about being an American soldier, about being entitled to the respect and honor that comes from having served, then you can lie about almost anything.

Now, scoundrels scramble headlong to the self-serving conclusion that, because the First Amendment protects a right to lie, then it *is* right to lie. Right? Logical?

The law limits some kinds of lying. Perjury and fraud are examples. But it's not a ball or a strike until an umpire calls it. Now the curve balls are coming in, and all night, too. The floodgates appear to be open wide, the floodlights up bright and 90 percent of what we hear all day long is the complete worst bullshit. Then another week goes by and sets a new low. Worse still, half of it, or much more, is roll-the-dice bullshit—that is to say, it is bullshit that is careless of its own consequences. But now we all expect it. And virtually none of it gets called out.

"The company has done absolutely everything it could possibly do to prevent the slurry leak."

"The company hadn't the slightest idea the drug caused deformities."

"We had no clue that the IUD ruined women's reproductive systems."

"I have never seen any science connecting tobacco to lung disease."

"Climate change is a hoax by China."

"I wanted to save my partner's feelings."

For the last thirty years, fossil fuel peddlers have been facing regulatory intervention on a massive scale. The stakes were higher than stakes had ever been, amounting to most of the profit remaining to be made, from 1980 to the end, by selling coal and oil to burn. That meant huge amounts of money were available to influence public opinion, particularly political opinion, to favor fossil fuel industries.

Exactly as with tobacco, extremely rewarding careers were made for the likes of Fred Singer, Tim Ball, and Christopher Monckton, aka the Third Viscount Monckton of Benchley—a troop of clowns if ever there was one. They and any other politicians and academics with thick enough crust could sell their souls to Old King Coal or his young prince, Big Oil, for a small bag of silver and, drinking for free, recycle the same contrived material as worked for the tobacco clowns. See Jim Hoggan's *Climate Cover-Up*.

"There is no proven connection between fossil fuels and climate change."

"Climate change is normal; it happens all the time."

"Clean coal is the fuel of the future."

"We're better off with 'ethical oil' from Canada than dirty oil from Arabs."

"We care about starvation and rape in Darfur, and we wish we could stop it."

"Al Gore drives cars, flies on jets and pays electrical bills, so his opinion about climate change is meaningless."

"There are some things you just don't say to your partner. I'll have mine on ice."

Business as usual, with the absolute minimum of discretionary decency.

And the bar has been lowered for what is acceptable human behavior. Well done, twentieth century; the marketplace was protected for irresponsible profiteering and human dignity was brought down a peg or two—all by a sneaky invisible hand.

But to blame this on corporations is self-deceptive avoidance. Corporations are the product of human laws. We ourselves and those that we elect to legislate on our behalf, to represent our interests in common, have failed completely in understanding our responsibility to regulate the behavior of these nonhuman legal persons we created. Our legislators are finely rewarded for defending corporate "freedom" over our common interests, including, incidentally, Universal Rights.

Of course shareholders, upon whose behalf corporations brush off atrocities to increase shareholder personal wealth, have a powerful selfish interest in keeping such regulation to a minimum. So they might use all the power and influence that comes with their Wealth to vigorously discourage any increase in regulation. *Dark Money*.

Then, when regulation is threatened at home, the corporation scampers to wherever such regulation, and regulators themselves, are for sale. They share hundreds of millions of dollars with leaders of tin pot republics, who then disregard all to protect handsome private profit. Corporate directors must do what their shareholders require of them, but we are not tripping over many shareholders proposing decency when it comes to toxic waste in Ecuador, slave conditions in gold mines and textile mills in Africa, or lethal leather tanning chemicals dumped in the drinking water of Mumbai's Dharavi slum. The estimated population of Dharavi is about a million, in five hundred acres. The drinking water there is a black puddle.

"Don't they get lots of rain there, dear? What are they called, mongoones? Isn't nature wonderful? Hope it rains for them lots. Shall I wear my soft pink or chartreuse leather to Crustacean?"

It's much more likely we'll rub shoulders with throngs of shareholders, "you can't see me" hands over their eyes, horny for the spoils of genocide, poisoning, deprivation and virtual slavery throughout the "Third World" and at least one other.

Corporations, as our agents, disregard and perpetrate atrocities, fund local robber barons and poison environments the world over on our behalf to advance our comforts and economies. We have a duty to regulate such behavior. Disregarding our responsibility and being complicit is not okay. Corporations are instruments of our creation. We can regulate them responsibly or throw up our hands in permissive surrender to our fateful truth. But there can be no one else to blame.

We have a fundamental responsibility to stand up for the victims of these atrocities perpetrated in our name and to our advantage. Our tenure on Earth is inexplicably miraculous, and it is our responsibility to protect it for all and pass it on, not to hog it now for our indefensibly greedy, thoughtless, selfish comfort.

When Adam Smith is relied upon by the likes of Milton Friedman, Ayn Rand and Stephen Harper to support the claim that self-interest ought to supersede moral responsibilities and our instinct to be good persons, he is both mis-taken and misrepresented. It is high time we wrestled human consciousness back from the clutches of these Pricks vainly trumpeting Smith's invisible hand to justify thoughtless self-interest, and restore to primacy what Smith insisted was the superior concept: natural human sympathy.

It is all the more our responsibility because this irresponsible minimalist decency of contemporary enterprise arises and occurs within the legal infrastructure that we provide, maintain and defend. Along with the unregulated corporation, that infrastructure also supports the most sacred cow of the primitive scoundrel: Sovereignty.

6

Sovereignty— Our Primitive Armor against Responsibility

This abuse of Sovereignty will die hard for the whingeing and braying of us all ... resisting awareness, refusing responsibility, denying complicity and disavowing receipt of any advantage from that abuse. That abuse, over there.

TEN THOUSAND years ago, 100,000 years ago, a big male stood before his people and put his foot down. He had control of his friends and all the tough guys, so as long as he successfully slaughtered all comers, Everything was His. There were no laws. He wasn't just the Cheese; He was the Whole Enchilada. *He was King*, and his every remark or impulsive gesture was the law.

Eventually, some kings proclaimed themselves God. It's fairly obvious, really.

"If I can render you wealthy or dead with a hitch of my brow, what's the difference? And anyway, who are you to say I am not a god ...?"

Soon, others were gods too, by heredity of course, or by sexual congress. Yes, some gods were even women. Sovereignty was said to have been granted by God, to have derived from Him as Divine Right. It came together with an absolute right to use and abuse all power in any way.

Increasingly, though, as does happen, gods met their neighbors. Africans, Goths, Gauls and Mongols all had their own ideas. Then gods, by the sheer weight of the overwhelming evidence of all likelihood, dwindled to be but kings again. Still, for us, the mere subjects, the answer to "Who are you to say?" remained the same.

"I'll shut up. That's who."

But there were certain "moral imperatives" upon a king—for example to look after his powerful circle of friends. And there were certain practical considerations—for example, keep your eldest son happy. If your eldest son killed you, he'd now be King and, thus, exactly as it was for His father before Him, even killing the King was no problem.

Kings learned to play by certain rules, to cooperate on certain terms, and came to arrangements among themselves, or they "got merged," either way. They each ran their protection businesses and called their turf "Nations" and their gangs of Nations "Empires." They looked after mutual interests as allies, including vanquishing all comers, whether from within by rebellion or from without by invasion.

Often, kings looked after the people they ruled. Quite evidently, there were good reasons to do so. People will fight sooner for the king who is beloved, and fight better too, than for the one who is cruel. Also, when people get rich, they pay taxes. You give them "protection," and they give you the juice, you know, the vig. It's a really good racket, always has been, and it is, actually, the oldest. The prostitution racket just doesn't work very well without the protection racket.

Funny, too, you can sell them your land, never mind that it's still your domain anyway. You get the sale money and you still get to tax their land and their income, and make all the rules. Win-win. For you. You are King.

Eventually, society began to chisel out certain rights for non-kings, too. By the time of the Magna Carta, they were using the Old French word "soverain." (1250–1300, Middle English, alteration by influence of reign < Old French soverain < Vulgar Latin *superānus, equivalent to Latin super- super- + -ānus -an—from Dictionary.com.) *Non potestis somniare sursum haec stercore, homo*—ask Google Translate.

Many of the advantages of sovereignty now extend to most of the people in the best country clubs, who before would have been mere subjects. The rights to travel in other Sovereign nations, to expect the protection of the law there and to be permitted the freedom to return home are all examples of agreements between sovereign nations for the benefit of their respective citizens. Particularly for those in country clubs. It is not that easy for a person from the slums of Dhaka to get a visa to Disneyland.

In our best Western country clubs, and a few others, we all live better now than most kings ever did. But in many other nations, it's "meet the new boss—same as the old boss." There, only kings (and their friends) live like kings, while all the rest scramble and tussle to take whatever spills off the royal table.

Among the historical appurtenances to sovereignty that now persist in our "modern" culture, the most inimical is the rote offering of respect to foreign sovereigns. Not only do we treat them with entirely undeserved respect, but it is no surprise to us that our corporations under such foreign rulers are forgiven the strictures of responsibility that we would thrust upon them were they at home. We know this perfectly well and still shrug it off without a moment's pause, because that's the way it is with sovereignty and enterprise.

Only Alberta, among the Western country clubs, permits free and unlimited dumping of ultra-toxic tar sands tailings in vast, lethal reservoirs on public land beside huge rivers of formerly fresh water that belong to the commons. In places like Ecuador, Nigeria, Indonesia, Kazakhstan and Chechnya, it is all very Albertan. There are no rules and the Privateers do as they please, as long as the king gets his cut. But the people are on their own when it comes to what's in their water. Win-win for the shareholders: huge oil profits, low royalties and no pesky human decency considerations about what Fort Chipewyan, downstream from the tar sands, drinks or eats.

"Clean up your mess."

"Yeah? Make me."

Multinational corporations fully use these "sovereign countries" (and one Canadian province) as resorts from the strictures of responsible regulation. Running their jurisdictions like thugs and idiots acting in complete disregard for the welfare of their people, these sovereign scoundrels permit our corporations to gurgitate all hell. Behind the armor of sovereignty, enterprises may perpetrate injustices that would be criminal atrocities in our country club, and so our corporations abroad have made deals with kings who wear black cowboy hats.

All the thugs don't wear black cowboy hats, only some in Nigeria and Alberta. Some wear costumes that make them look like Eddie Murphy in *Coming to America*; others don military regalia so ridiculously encrusted with baubles and ribbons as to make a Soviet general raise his prodigious brow in envy. Some just look like they're from Edmonton.

These thuggish clowns have one thing they share: the claim of sovereignty. It provides Shell with all the Royal excuse a Dutch company needs to utterly disregard the gangsterism, exploitation and ruthless self-interested hijacking of their host country's common resources for Privateers' personal profit with absolutely no regard for the slightest human decency. And a good thing it is, too, because such human decency does very little for the Royal Dutch bottom line. Or their pimp hosts.

A person asks, "What can you tell us of the four hundred young women kidnapped where you are working in Nigeria?"

Shell, a nonhuman legal person, responds, "When we are in Nigeria, or any foreign nation, we have a responsibility as guests and as

representatives of our shareholders to not inter-
fere in our hosts' domestic affairs."

Yes, but you pay them hundreds of millions
in royalties. They are cozy with you; they
relax and remove all responsible regulation.
They must feel some pressure to be responsive
to your humanitarian concerns. What do you
think is happening to those young women
today, now?

"We most certainly do not agree with your
emotional characterization. It's preposterous
to think that we have any business whatsoever
interfering in the internal affairs of our host
nation. We are as concerned as anyone about
the safety of the girls, and we pray for their safe
return."

You sit with these men daily. They are rich on
your royalties. Do you have no influence?

"We did not enter into a development agree-
ment with Nigeria so that we could make the
ridiculous presumption of interfering in their
domestic affairs. Nigeria is a Sovereign nation."

You eat dinner with them.

"We have discussed these problems in a
friendly way, and we are satisfied that the guy in
the black cowboy hat is doing absolutely everything he can to bring about a resolution to this
difficult situation."

Do you think the young women are being raped now? Do you have granddaughters that age?

"Your hysterical questions are impertinent. We completely fulfill our duties as a foreign corporation visiting in Nigeria."

Now Americans, Russians, other Europeans and many others run across borders and do whatever they have to do to get what they want. Then they run back home knowing no Lone Ranger will be coming after *them*.

In 2017, shareholders world round will be very pleased with the performance of their corporate representative directors.

Sovereignty is all the excuse shareholders need to utterly disregard the true costs of their increasing net worth. Shareholders the world over—teachers' and nurses' pension funds, mutual funds, life insurance companies and banks—all need never consider how many chemicals are dumped, how many people are driven off their land, what human rights are violated or workers rights disregarded, or how much collateral damage is inflicted, whether by Boko Haram, the Janjaweed, Bashar al-Assad's Alawite Ba'ath Party or Uncle Sam. Dividends will still be declared.

Former president of Nigeria Goodluck Jonathan need not worry about *his* royalties.

They will be forthcoming no matter how long the four hundred young women are held and raped. Talisman's Albertan and other shareholders may feel the same assurance about their Darfur dividends. The Gold Medal Cheater Vladimir Putin's shares in Bashar al-Assad's gas pipelines remain intact. Rex Tillerson and Exxon are pleased to help Putin and al-Assad make money killing and displacing millions of victims and refugees. That's business. Tar sands investors are very grateful to future Albertans for the free dumping of toxic waste.

All abuse of Universal Rights, or Responsibilities of Freedom disavowed, by claim of sovereignty, or any other mockery, will have three elements: the Pricks, their Help and those Abused. Pricks perpetrate the abuse. Their Help are all who work for, buy from or sell to, invest in, profit from or otherwise benefit from the advantage taken by Pricks; thus, they are themselves Pricks Designate by the rubbing of shoulders. In another word: "Us." Country clubs are filled with Us Pricks and Pricks Designate. The Abused are kept out of our sovereign Western country club by our velvet rope.

This abuse of sovereignty will die hard for the whingeing and braying of us all, Pricks and Pricks Designate alike, resisting awareness, refusing responsibility, denying complicity and disavowing receipt of any advantage from that abuse. That abuse, over there.

Sovereignty serves us well, contributing in many ways to world order, but we must not permit it to provide refuge for the conduct of criminal irresponsibility or for the masking of its proceeds. It must not be put to the use of scoundrels as an instrument of deprivation, nor may it any longer serve as our armor against stakeholder awareness and responsibility.

The corporations' duty to behave with the minimum of human decency and our abject ambivalence to their responsible regulation, together with sovereignty, have bought a life of luxury for a fifth of the world, comfort for another third, and for all the remainder, conditions that for us in our country clubs would be an utter nonstarter, ranging from subsistence and degradation to squalor.

But sovereignty must not excuse oppression. We now know that in our democratic heritage, the heir to the Sovereign is the people. There is a point where a Sovereign gets so bad that the Good Heir has the responsibility to step into their place, and where there is no functioning democracy, rebellion is the time-honored remedy for such abuse. America need only remember.

Some things must trump Sovereignty. They include Universal Rights and the conservation of the commons, the natural bounty that has befallen us all. Divine right does not reside in a Sovereign but in us all. Same as divine responsibility. A knight must save a maiden. There is a reason. He owes his Freedom to the people and is bound by goodness to pay the debt.

Another very difficult obstacle to fulfilling our duties as beneficiaries of Freedom and Universal Rights is the greed of, and abuse of power by, Pricks. Those of us who cannot elevate ourselves above that level will not come along unless made to do so.

7

The Sword— Responsibility Enforced

O! it is excellent
To have a giant's strength, but it is tyrannous
To use it like a giant.

MEASURE FOR MEASURE
WILLIAM SHAKESPEARE

WHERE THERE is a right, there must also be a duty to accord the right. In our society, we properly expect that duty to be fulfilled by our law through courts and our other institutions of government. It implies the right—moreover, the obligation—of enforcement against any who would repudiate or diminish another's right. We begin with civil procedure or police intervention, intensifying as required, ultimately until court order or arrest. We expect it. We are entitled to the protection of our rights as citizens. And we take it for granted, as surely as we take for granted that it's good for our kids to be doctors and lawyers.

Most of the time, as this culture of Rights and Responsibilities that I recommend unfolds, and as such law emerges, people will follow the law. But when they do not, when innocent lives or any other rights, including Universal Rights, are at stake, though the pen is mightier than the sword, it is mighty much more slowly, often catastrophically slowly. If one looked only at Rwanda, one would need look no further. Events frequently require justice to be realized more swiftly than the pen can bring off. In that moment, the Sword spared is our duty failed.

In recent history, that Sword—the application of force to require responsibility—includes less overtly violent forces, such as enacting economic sanctions, freezing assets, and denying travel or access to our banking systems. We are, in varying degrees, less reluctant to apply the Sword in these, its more genteel forms. It is at the point of application of violent force that we are reluctant, but very often our proper reluctance must be overridden by duty.

Goodness cannot emerge if evil is not suppressed. (Ibid.) Justice merely demanded virtually always comes excessively late. In the critical moment, pacifism ought to be an ideal, but it must not be our prime motivation, or we will fail utterly and constantly in our responsibility to victims. It would be odd, at least, to depend upon only pacifism when the evil gun is at the head of the innocent child.

We must not feel joy or righteousness in the power of our responsibility. It is no thing to celebrate. But sometimes, if people threaten and will not desist, they must be stopped by force, or even killed. This is a horror, there is nothing happy in it. One might well cringe at the image of Christians laughing and cheering at the killing of bin Laden. But that does not diminish the responsibility that has befallen us as the beneficiaries of Freedom and Universal Rights whereby we are duty bound.

If someone does not accept and respect the Responsibilities of their Freedom or everyone's Universal Rights, then we have a responsibility against *them* to that extent. That responsibility would instantly become meaningless without it being imposed—if necessary, by force. We certainly expect it within our country club.

We demand that the Sword be brandished at home, where we regard it as law enforcement. At home, we are comfortable with force being swiftly and wisely applied to immediately end a dangerous transgression. Indeed, our peace and security at home are the direct fruit of exactly such a systemic enforcement of rights.

But across a national border, we think of it
as another matter, something more sinister.
We call it war. And most often, we object to international intervention for years, or forever, no
matter how gross the injustice perpetrated,
how vast the number slaughtered, because we
do not hold with the imposition of violent force.
Except to satisfy our feeling of entitlement to
the protection of *our own* rights.

But why is our responsibility to protect the
rights of innocent people extinguished at a
border, when circumstances cry out for their
protection on the other side of the line? It seems
to me such extinguishment cannot be taken
for granted.

If four hundred of our adolescent girls were
kidnapped from our neighborhood school and
raped, protestors would not stand in the way
of the police with signs demanding an end to
imperialist aggression or chanting, "Give peace
a chance." We require neither pacifism nor
due process under multilateral treaties when it
happens to us at home.

On our side of the boundary, we might feel
like accomplices if we do not intervene on behalf
of a victim, but on the other side of the border,
we are somehow comfortably complicit, thinking
Sovereignty protects us from responsibility. Do

we think we are sparing the world interventions by force? Then why do we demand interventions by force at home?

Having considered Sovereignty, we see it is double-edged. While protecting our proper self-determination, all too often it also protects despicable irresponsibility that we would recognize as our duty to suppress were it occurring within our country club. And so, if we seek reasons for not crossing the foreign border to enforce Universal Rights, Sovereignty does not pass the test. We know that Sovereignty must not be used to protect or mask abuse of Universal Rights, so neither can it be used properly to excuse ourselves of the responsibility to protect the innocent anywhere. The shield of Sovereignty does not withstand the Sword of Universal Rights. Those who depend on Sovereignty as their last excuse for abusing Universal Rights must expect enforcement. Banditos may expect Kemosabe to come plunging through the Rio Grande in Silver's galloping splash. Whether at home or away, Justice is our duty and our highest responsibility.

Our courts know very well how to consider such issues, and good law will emerge as quickly as we are bright enough for it to occur to us and to make the case in court. When it occurs in a jurisdiction where the victims have no recourse to courts, that is where our dire, unavoidable responsibility remains to be fulfilled.

Let those who tempt Justice to take up her Sword be shown and shown well. She has been turned loose among us, but in only a limited way. And small minds have often turned her Sword to their small ends. But Justice is neither small, nor is she finished.

If we hope to teach respect for Rights and Responsibilities, we must show respect. No abuse that calls upon itself the Sword of Justice must be excused, either at home or abroad.

We are quite properly averse to war that is based upon selfish interests, such as political or economic imperialism. When somebody else commits that error, though, we have little choice. Of course, we are quite rightly averse to war as well because it costs the lives of "our" soldiers. However, although our hearts are rent by injury or death of police officers, we are decidedly not averse to asking of them the ultimate sacrifice at home as a last resort. In our domestic policing situations, not only do we take it for granted, we demand it.

Perhaps our aversion to war also comes partly from the implacable reality of collateral damage, the killing of innocents who happen to be in harm's way when the shit hits the fan. We tend not to dwell upon it precisely because it is as unjust as it is unavoidable. Like tinnitus in rock musicians, collateral damage is not much spoken about in public.

Collateral damage occurs now primarily from bombing. It is that very nature of bombing that rightly makes it virtually unheard of as a tactic in domestic police enforcement. Bombing in war is precisely our attempt to use force against enemies by sacrificing innocent civilian lives rather than putting our own soldiers in harm's way. When those innocents are our fellow citizens, we will have no part of bombing. But when they are "others" the world over, it's bombs away. Not only are we failing in our duty to protect these innocents and their Universal Rights, we are writing them off to reduce our costs of living easy.

"Precision bombing" is a fictitious construct, like "clean coal." It must be very difficult indeed for a person in the president's position to be at peace with this. They must prefer the deaths of innocent people by bombing to risking the lives of our own soldiers on the ground.

But Sovereignty is not alone as an unacceptable excuse against the Sword of Justice. There is also the abuse at home, by those to whom we have entrusted the authority to enforce Justice, by their failure to draw her Sword upon themselves. The Sword is not entrusted to those in authority to be used (or not used) to further their personal interests. Extraordinary Influence may not be abused by its trustee to their personal advantage where any other person's Freedom or Universal Rights are diminished as a consequence. If abusers will not stop themselves, then they must be stopped by force.

Dick Cheney and his fellow purveyors of torture enjoy a distinct advantage arising directly from this conundrum of morality seen in President Obama's drone bombs. Former president George W. Bush, his vice-president, Dick Cheney, and his secretary of defense, Donald Rumsfeld, have not been prosecuted for their criminal use of torture in part because, if a president or vice-president can be prosecuted for torture, then surely presidents can also be prosecuted for intentionally bombing innocent people. It is for these reasons exactly that Uncle Sam will not submit to the jurisdiction of the International Criminal Court.

Torture and the bombing of civilians both are deployed for no better reason than to advance political objectives, to avoid the appearance of failure, where fair play comes only at much higher political cost.

As Duke Vincentio says in Shakespeare's *Measure for Measure*, "He who the sword of heaven will bear/Should be as holy as severe... Shame to him whose cruel striking/kills for faults of his own liking!"

So if not "upon faults of our own liking" (in another word, "arbitrarily"), then upon what faults *is* it our duty to brandish the Sword? I propose that the Responsibilities of Freedom and Universal Rights be our guides. The Sword of enforcement must be taken up across international boundaries and across domestic boundaries of power alike, if we are to live up to our duty.

It so happens Jesus of Nazareth considered this circumstance and shared his view quite clearly. According to the Gospel of Thomas (found in Egypt about the same time the Dead Sea Scrolls were discovered in what is now the West Bank), Jesus said: "The kingdom of the father is like a certain man who wanted to kill a powerful man. In his own house he drew his sword and stuck it into the wall in order to find out whether his hand could carry through. Then he slew the powerful man" (Thomas, 98).

It's little wonder this bit never made it
into the gospels sanctioned by Rome (ironically, Rome's editing here was unquestioningly
adopted by born-again Christianity). It wouldn't
help the power structures much, Jesus letting
forth parables about slaying the powerful. Still,
it seems that, sometimes, powerful men need to
be brought to Justice even by the sword. President Obama may well have gone to church very
much at peace with his Lord, were it not for the
collateral damage wrought by his drone bombs.

Obama should have used the authority
entrusted to him and turned the Sword of Justice
upon the perpetrators of torture and of collateral
damage. He should favor the indictment of
George W. Bush and Donald Rumsfeld for
sanctioning criminal torture. And having left
office, he should personally surrender to the
jurisdiction of the International Criminal Court
and petition that court to prosecute him for
the war crime of knowingly and intentionally
causing the deaths of innocent bystanders. He
should admit his guilt and submit to the mercy
of Justice before the whole world. This would be
his way to show respect both for the law and for
the authority entrusted to him.

Then he would be regarded as more than
a great president. In history, he would stand

shoulder to shoulder with Mahatma Gandhi and Nelson Mandela, with Abraham Lincoln and Martin Luther King. Like Muhammad Ali, he would be the greatest. Like Christ.

This is how the trustee of the Sword of Justice earns the status and respect to stand up against abusers of Freedom and Universal Rights everywhere.

8

Justice and Liberty—The Base and Measure of Democracy

What Justice and Liberty need is nice wheels.
They need to get around a lot more.

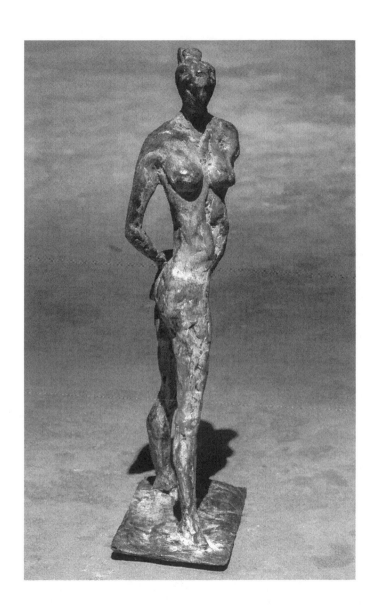

IN HER LEFT hand, she holds her Sword. But in her right hand, Justice holds Scales so that she may measure more carefully all ifs and buts. In one tray go the facts, and in the other go Universal Rights and the Responsibilities of Freedom. These must weigh most heavily in the Scales of Justice.

Freedom means exactly what every member of our country club presumes it means. It is a complex of Rights and Responsibilities. We are safe and secure in our person and our property to go where we like in the commons; to earn income; and to secure food, clothing and shelter. We have access to education, to health care, to basic capital and to Justice. And we have, at least to some degree, a clean environment.

Freedom and Justice (Rights) do not come without a cost. Their cost is Responsibility. All who have had Freedom and Rights befall them owe the duty to strive for the same to befall all others as well.

Most of us largely fulfill the Responsibilities of our Rights and Freedoms, at least within our own country club. We pay the proper costs when we pay taxes that support our institutions of democracy. Not only is it a responsibility, but it is an honor and a privilege to support these democratic institutions by paying taxes. It is our schools, police departments, courts, legislatures, military and hospitals that establish and protect our Rights and Freedoms. Each time we object to paying our taxes, we fail in our responsibility and dishonor our duty. We also pay our dues when we call out those who deny their duty and decline to pay.

And lastly, we pay the proper costs of the Freedom that has befallen us every time we acknowledge, stand up for, promote and strive to fulfill our responsibilities to accord Universal Rights and Freedom to All.

As well as her Scales and her Sword, Justice has a blindfold so that she can neither favor the rich and powerful nor disfavor the poor or humble, though at first, somehow, her blindfold was askew and did permit her to distinguish by race and gender. Legislators never had such blindfolds, nor did crooked police. Perhaps Justice should take off her blindfold, if only to protect us from selfish legislators and to watch crooked cops.

She might take off her blindfold for another good reason. What Justice needs is nice wheels. She needs to get around a lot more. She should get nice wheels with lots of room, like a ragtop Coupe De Ville, so that Liberty may ride along shotgun. Together with Justice's Sword and Scales, there must be room in the trunk for Liberty's Light and Book. Liberty holds her Light so that all may see her show the way. And she carries her Book, inscribed upon it the date that she arrived in America. It is her Book of Account, setting out the proper cost of Liberty and her ledger of payments due, because this lady is neither free nor cheap. Presently, it is a very thick book of account, mostly because of her receivables.

Justice and Liberty are not just statues to remain in their place. They should both get around a lot more. And it is our duty to help them.

They must go to Africa, where millions are starving while the rich and powerful take all the oil and everything else from above or under the ground. They take all the arable land and hoard the food for only those with money to buy. Across Africa, Justice and Liberty would be welcomed in many places as strangers.

Justice and Liberty must go east, through the desert kingdoms, and north, through the steppes and the cold, dark forests. They need to cross the mountains to the teeming masses on both sides of the Himalayas.

Then, after being away, Liberty and Justice might return to America and be properly recognized there for the first time, for what they really are, the birthright of us all, all of us everywhere.

Justice and Liberty had better be given safe passage, because they are Earth's most important citizens. If they are not yet yours, they will be soon. If we are wise, honest and responsible, we will be sure to help them on their way. They are the personification of our Rights and Responsibilities. And before long, the date they came to your country will be inscribed in Liberty's book, too.

As much as it is our responsibility to extend Justice and Liberty to all, this is also the way we properly celebrate them both. It is not their fault that America, in so many ways, has sullied their reputations, reputations that shall be restored to them as they are shown off to the whole world.

We admire and proclaim Justice and Liberty because we think they are good. The absence or diminishment of either is bad. If it is bad for any of us, it is so for all. And we struggle with our institutions of democracy against that badness. Goodness is our reason.

Well, good then. Goodness.

What is that?

What Good Is Goodness?

It comes down to basic schoolyard wisdom: whether you are a good guy who can sleep at night or a selfish asshole, up pacing the bedroom floor of your soul.

ETHICS IS the philosophy of right and wrong conduct, of good and evil. It is always difficult to regard ethics honestly, but it is especially difficult when, like most of us, you have done wrong. Perhaps that is part of the reason ethics have fallen off the pop radar.

That scientists are paid some regard in Canada was demonstrated by their muzzling by former prime minister Stephen Harper. Why muzzle what you do not fear? Lawyers are regarded, distinguished and then disregarded by opposing lawyers. But ethicists are not even disregarded. They could walk through the room and it would be like nothing happened. A rabbi, a priest and a minister could walk into the bar with an ethicist and it would still be a normal joke.

Ethics, besides being evident to every kid in second grade, embody a branch of philosophy that is, similar to epistemology and jurisprudence, more honored now in the breach, if at all—as opposed to logic, which receives interminable lip service.

Right and wrong are judgments even kids can make. Often they make judgments on the basis of ideas of good and evil. It's good for big guys to look out for little guys. It's evil for big guys, or gangs of little ones, to be pricks and bullies. While we proceed in this enquiry, I hope that we will keep in mind, at least, what is evident to every kid in second grade. Never mind that when they get beyond the schoolyard, things look, well, different.

It seems natural for us to prefer goodness over badness. Good stuff is better than bad stuff; being treated well is better than being treated like shit. With a bit of time, the kid realizes that his sister's feelings are pretty much the same as his. With but a tiny leap more of imagination, he'll recognize the same thing about his friend's sister, too. Before long, we become civilized— that is, we recognize the equal expectations of us all, and treat others the way we would like to be treated. When we consider ethics in our reasons for action, and even when we don't, goodness is a quality that is, itself, sufficient reason for our choices.

There is good reason to prefer good. Good things work the best, last the longest and just feel right. Bad things work the worst, except in the short term; they last their owner for the least time and they feel shitty. Bad things just feel shitty. I can't explain it.

It's just like human behavior. Good behavior works best, lasts the longest and just feels right. Bad behavior is bad for everybody, except, in the short term, for its perpetrator. Whatever advantage comes of bad behavior is short-lived and feels so bad you have to drink, fight and change friends frequently to enjoy yourself even a little. It comes down to basic schoolyard wisdom: whether you are a good guy who can sleep at night or a selfish asshole, up pacing the bedroom floor of your soul.

A bit like our neighbors in the Universe, we too have had much experience with the letting of evil run wild. It is why we established institutions to protect our Rights and Freedom in our country clubs. But as we wander in the darker corners of our school grounds, or off the grounds entirely, our sense of right and wrong is constantly affronted. Precision bombs terrorize and obliterate innocent children every day. Signs that say "Private Property" separate the starving from vast amounts of what they need to stay alive. The food we waste and throw away would nourish a billion people daily. (Ibid.)

Messes like the tar sands tailings ponds (more like Great Lakes) are left behind without a backward glance, questions about who will clean them up hardly rating a shrug. Until the task falls to the taxpayer. Let the Beaver Lake Cree eat exotic toxins in their fish and game. Let them drink poisoned water. That's the taste of other people making money. What value is there in an ethic that permits such results? Plenty of value for tar sands Pricks. Not so much for their Fort Chip First Nations hosts, eh?

Corporations and individuals alike blithely toss ethics utterly aside when they're provided with solid arguments designed to suit the convenience of selfish interests. Arguments like "sovereignty," "a free marketplace unfettered by regulation," "private property," "Clean up our own backyard first." And, in some quarters, arguments like "Go fuck yourself" are offered in support of rapacious selfishness running wild.

If we are to take our Responsibilities of Freedom and of Universal Rights seriously, including the obligation to conserve our natural bounty, we are required to consider ceaselessly the good of others. Our obligations require us to weigh and measure competing views of "good." They require us to practice ethics. Our institutions are built on the premise and with the intention that they will ensure our common good—a difficult task without knowing how to properly recognize that good.

To succeed ultimately, our institutions need only one thing more. Their terms of reference must expand from *our* common good to *the* common good. We must no longer be, like the founding fathers of American independence, insistent upon our own rights but somewhat less concerned with those of our slaves and women. The women in the ragtop Coupe De Ville need to get around to every one of us, everywhere. Justice and Liberty, if they embrace any of us, must soon embrace us all. America dreamed the right dream, just in an un-stereotypically piddly way.

It wouldn't cost any more than our global "defense" budget. Moreover, people who are cared for don't bust our balls. It's called Sympathy. Although 250 years ago Adam Smith thought we might recognize it in everybody (and Christ

1,700 years before him), Sympathy has become more a stranger since Henry Kissinger rationalized, "America has no permanent friends or enemies, only interests." What is the nature of sympathy that we shouldn't just disregard it as a useless sentimental artifact from our history? Like ethics? Or friendships?

Sympathy

Why would we not be sympathetic? We are the same. We are the same thing: conscious creatures, the Universe's vessels of consciousness.

ADAM SMITH'S *Theory of Moral Sentiments* is not quoted as much as his *Wealth of Nations* (though he thought the former considerably superior). And it is little wonder why. *Moral Sentiments* makes a remarkable presumption about humans that all but obliterates Smith's usefulness as a defender of selfishness. His favorite work begins:

> How selfish soever man may be supposed, there are evidently some principles in his nature, which interest him in the fortunes of others, and render their happiness necessary to him, though he derives nothing from it, except the pleasure of seeing it. Of this kind is pity or compassion, the emotion we feel for the misery of others, when

we either see it, or are made to conceive it in a very lively manner. That we often derive sorrow from the sorrows of others, *is a matter of fact too obvious to require any instances to prove it*; for this sentiment, like all the other original passions of human nature, is by no means confined to the virtuous or the humane, though *they perhaps may feel it with the most exquisite sensibility.* The greatest ruffian, the most hardened violator of the laws of society, is not altogether without it. (emphasis added)

This philosopher, who is now most often relied upon to support the proposition that we need only pursue our own self-interest, identifies principles in our nature that interest us in the well-being of others for nothing in return except the pleasure of seeing it.

He called it Sympathy, he attributed it to us all and he expected us to find it as much in the rich or mean-spirited as in anybody.

Perhaps another instance of this kind of sympathy in our nature is what we call love. We popularly celebrated such love when I was young. Curiously, it was Smith who most clearly set out the vision for our dawning age. Although Milton Friedman, Ayn Rand, Spiro Agnew and Fred Trump misrepresent him in vain defense of selfishness, Smith observed:

The rich only select from the heap what is most precious and agreeable. They consume little more than the poor, and in spite of their natural selfishness and rapacity, though they mean only their own conveniency, though the sole end which they propose from the labours of all the thousands whom they employ be the gratification of their own vain and insatiable desires, *they divide with the poor the produce of all their improvements. They are led by an invisible hand to make nearly the same distribution of the necessaries of life, which would have been made, had the earth been divided into equal portions among all its inhabitants,* and thus without intending it, without knowing it, advance the interest of the society, and afford means to the multiplication of the species. (emphasis added)

The rich take the best, but they can't really eat too much more than the poor. Despite their selfish appetites, and although they only intend to indulge their own insatiable desires, still, they share with the poor. They are led by an invisible hand to share, as if "the earth had been divided into equal portions among all its inhabitants." So before "the invisible hand" had ever received the qualifier "of the free market" from its voracious proponents, there it was, through human

sympathy, inspiring the rich to share, magnificently, with the poor.

Smith's vision bears precious little resem-
blance to the pretense he is now alleged to
support, much the same way Jesus is now being
called upon to justify prejudice and bigotry
against most sexual orientations, Muslims,
liberals and atheists, to name sadly few. Smith's
sympathy, in full context and not merely cherry-
picked, actually supports more naturally a
commonality based upon peace, love, understanding and sharing.

For instance, when I was much younger, in
Calgary, in a row of houses on Memorial Drive
across from the Bow River parklands, dwelt hip-
pies. Frank Hoggan was a classic of the period.
He had a house on Memorial, and it was known
to be a place where a new way of looking at the
Universe, and our place in it, was available at
less than five bucks. Frank didn't have much
affinity for the psychedelic experience himself,
but he enjoyed the company. And he enjoyed
lots of beer. We called guys like Frank beer-
heads. His brother, Jim, who lived with him, was
an influence of a different kind. Jim Hoggan has
emerged as a highly regarded writer and speaker
on communicating effectively in difficult areas
that have become adversarial—for example,

climate change. However, in 1969, Jim was the first person that I ever noticed use a peculiar word. It was in the title of a book he gave me: *The Way of Zen*, by Alan Watts. Jim gave me another book, by a strange fellow named Hermann Hesse, called *Siddhartha*. They seemed sort of beatnik.

During the (belated in Canada) Summer of Love, there were lots of consciousness catalysts and empathy elaborators around. Zen rang a bell for me. I was knocked out by the compelling vastness to be found in every moment of doing absolutely nothing, but doing it vigilantly. Now I know even more completely the worth of that hunch. Watts, Hesse and Jim seemed to get it all, in an instant. It flows through all of us, an unending, brilliant welling up of awareness. Be still, yet still be. Alive to all instants. You can't get richer than that. A drunkard's dream. All you need do to get more than you ever dared dream is sweet fuck all. The sound of one hand clapping.

I was all in, John of the Crossroads stirred like a medieval holy man, hearing from on high the universe speak one word from all eternity, a word spoken in eternal silence and in that silence still to be heard. (Apologies, St. John of the Cross.)

It had occurred to me once, while pretty much embracing a tree, that I could feel the life coursing through it. It seemed to me that the tree could sense me as well—either way, it, too, was alive. Wind blew through our leaves and our hair. It was miraculous and it was everywhere.

Tiny seeds take up the elements air, water, soil and sunshine, then organize them into whole new participants altogether, new makers of seeds, huge, regenerative, reproducing beings. And if trees aren't astonishing enough, what about the deer that walk among the trees, or even more, the birds that perch in them singing, and then, when they care to, fly free?

How astonishing is a human child who can dream dreams, and then make them real?

And what about this very being, so filled with astonishment? What is this instantiation of awareness we think of as our "self"?

The inescapable fact that such creatures exist at all—and that by some miracle, we are, each of us, of that unique type that can dream, wonder, understand, explain and, possibly above all, though utterly deaf, write a Ninth Symphony— was so extravagantly magnificent and filled one with such proper astonishment that the very dawning of the awareness might quite naturally have brought a welling up. All life is made out of the same stuff, yet we have that inexplicable additional magic, that we "perhaps may feel it with the most exquisite sensibility."

At that time, there were some fables turning up in the popular press pronouncing acid an escape from reality. But, on the incisive contrary, the experience of embracing the tree was, if anything, an escape *to* reality. We may quite properly be filled full, and to overflowing, with joy in every moment we live, in sheer breathlessness at life's fugitive nature, its capacity for anguish and ecstasy, disappointment and appointment. But if we swelled with emotion and welled with tears of astonishment every time we came upon a tree or met a child in the street—well, we'd never get into the fucking office.

As sure as we have to step back from our rapture or anguish enough to get things done, we have also learned to habitually, instantaneously tamp down these wellings-up at their faintest first hint so that they will not overtake us and betray us to our fellows, who would be afraid we had lost our shit.

"Act like a man. Get real."

Right?

I don't think so. No, stepping back from rapture or anguish, though necessary for certain social or personal reasons, is more likely to be a step away from our true nature than one toward it. Disregarding our proper astonishment, as we do moment to moment to "get along," is the actual escape from reality, our reality of abounding wonder and mystery that, by some magic, continues.

We decided to explore this insight exceedingly, and discover what it means to be a conscious being in the Universe, what it must really mean, which does not always accord easily with what we were taught as children. It was not merely permissible to be overflowing with astonishment. It was even more than a right. It was a responsibility to ourselves and to all others, as conscious creatures in the Universe, to embrace, enfold and exalt such *proper astonishment* so that we might share it the better with all whom we encounter. Sympathy indeed. Sympathy may be the least of it.

When I was a child, I learned to say the rosary at Grandma and Grandpa's house. The family would get on their knees in the living room (well, at least one knee), usually resting an elbow against the arm of a couch or chair. Each with our own holy rosary, we would recite the prayers in order, as the beads dictate. The main thing is the Hail Mary, which is repeated fifty times, ten times each in five decades. The next most frequent prayer is the Glory Be, which ends with the "doxology," the short hymn of praise to God: "As it was in the beginning, is now and ever shall be, world without end. Amen." It's also beautiful in the Latin: *Sicut erat in principio, et nunc, et semper, et in saecula saeculorum. Amen.*

Since childhood, I had been truly awash in eternity and in infinity, among angels, with a certain all-powerful eternal being, above, looking out for me, and for all of us. In the infinite Universe abided eternal all-loving, all-knowing perfection.

Arthur C. Clarke wrote the story, and Stanley Kubrick made the moving picture, but "if there's no audience, there just ain't no show" (thanks, Bill Henderson). And we were *all* set in 1969 to see in *2001: A Space Odyssey* the eternal fetus arising, vastly at peace, pure love floating infinitely among the stars. And in the mirror.

On black-and-white television, I watched a child wailing in fear and anguish on the war-torn streets of Hanoi in Vietnam. And I knew there was no difference between that child and me. Any distinction had to do with our experience, not with our selves.

Jesus said, "The man old in days will not hesitate to ask a small child seven days old about the place of life, and he will live. For many who are first will become last, and they will become one and the same" (Thomas 4).

Why would we not be sympathetic? We are the same. We are the same thing: conscious creatures, the Universe's vessels of consciousness. Dare we grasp and embrace the implications of this? Or are we so special we may disregard that child? What are the limits of our Sympathy? What should they be?

Perhaps in this light we might consider a place like India.

Now Take India

What is it to recognize a situation then disregard it? Do we recognize our ignorance of human degradation? Are we even vaguely familiar?

WHEN MY friends and I arrived in New Delhi in 2005, I was the only one of us somewhat accustomed to India.

There are two classes of everything in India. The best is called "export quality." Then there is what everybody else affords if they can. Jim Hoggan had been in Rishikesh, a city northeast of New Delhi, which is pretty much all export quality. From the world over, aspiring yogis and other seekers throng there to numerous world-famous ashrams, including that of Maharishi Mahesh Yogi, where Jim had been a familiar in the seventies. But Rishikesh is like the San Miguel de Allende of India—that is, hardly exemplary of society there generally, and Jim had never spent much time where the people of India shit in the street.

So I suggested that on our first day we stroll up the streets of Old Delhi from the Red Fort, two miles to the other end of Chandni Chowk market, sometimes on the jammed and jangling boulevard, but also along the winding vastness of side streets no wider than hallways, lined with closet-sized businesses. We could hardly see the sky because the air was so filled with the wires of pirated electricity, yet, still, the air we breathed was frequently clouded to choking by generator smoke. The garlanded dead lay in the tiny streets, politely bowed to by passersby, awaiting their stretcher to the freeing funeral pyre.

People, a million at a time in endless succession, swarmed the boulevard daily to acquire or provide goods decidedly not of export quality but rather ranging from the dishearteningly domestic to the miserable. The crowd was so relentless as to assure that we need not worry about moving anywhere quickly.

Along Chandni Chowk, children with snot-caked fingers and faces, all blackened like the kohled eyes of their baby sisters, poked and grabbed. Unless we were stern. But how can any feeling person possibly be stern in the face of such impoverishment? I gathered my friends for a quick huddle and told them what I had learned another time.

Fifteen years before, while shopping for leathers on the other side of the city, near Connaught Circus in New Delhi, quite evidently a less humble side of town, I met a young woman who was nursing an infant. She looked to be about thirty but was probably eighteen. Mother's milk adorned her saffron sari on both sides. She was selling crude tourist maps at five rupees, which was, then, about fifteen cents. I bought one and paid her fifty rupees, thinking I would help her and her son. I was immediately set upon by a dozen other women who cried, "I have children too, give me fifty rupees!"

Rafik was a young Kashmiri man who hustled tourists, telling them they must come to "his uncle's shop." Of course, his uncle was any shop owner who would pay the pittance bird dogs like Rafik received.

A day after I had "helped" the young mother, she and Rafik were in that same market area. She saw me talking with Rafik, approached us and asked Rafik if he would translate to me.

The woman told me that *all* money I gave her went to the beggar-pimp who held the franchise for that block. Much of the money taken from her by that pimp went to the corner cop. If the woman brought in 50 rupees ($1.50) in a day, she was given 2 rupees (6 cents). All people who begged or hustled but did not remit were violently beaten and had everything taken from them. Nobody refused to pay the cop.

The best corners had the best beggars. And the richest cops. People with crippling defects were at every corner, some by birth but many more, it is said, by reengineering after birth, the better a beggar-career to be had. Wasn't it better to have one hand with some money than to be starving with two hands empty?

She said that if I really wanted to help her, and I did, the best I could do was buy T-shirts and shorts for her infant. The beggar-pimp and cop had less interest in such things.

That night, as I walked to my hotel at about 2 AM, I saw the woman, among innumerable others, lying asleep on the sidewalk. She lay on her side, her left breast falling free. Her infant son lay on his back beside her, arms and legs splayed widely in his new outfit—red shorts with white piping and a white T-shirt—mother's breast to his lips. He suckled unconsciously, sleeping happily.

As it was for beggars then, across town in Connaught Circus, so it was this day in Chandni Chowk with my little-prepared company. It became much less unsettling for my friends, Enid, Geoff and Jim alike, to deny the children their alms, knowing they were depriving beggar-pimps and cops more than they were disappointing the kids. Of course, the kids knew that, too. Once it was clear that we knew the score, they laughed and carried on to torment others. Still, visitors may well find themselves off balance. Even knowing that it is not them who deprive these children, still the children remain impoverished. Those who take, do take all, and then let the children sleep by the gutter for their trouble.

People tried to sell small bits of waste lumber, chopped braids of hair, old punctured inner tubes and pieces of string. Lepers and others with open sores were utterly disregarded by the throng. Single barefoot men pushed loads on carts that would fill a three-quarter-ton pickup, and women carried bales of bricks upon their heads.

Unlike Connaught Circus, here in Chandni Chowk there were no cars, no trousers nor ties. The few most fortunate were dressed in a tidy pajama set or sari. Most were in rags the same color as the dirt in which we all walked, more than half of us in bare feet. Twenty-five thousand choking three-wheel put-puts, each carrying too many passengers, jerked and honked, pointed up one side or down the other of the ancient boulevard as if they intended to get anywhere at all through the whole vast, mesmerizing clamor of jostling, teeming insufficiency.

At the T-intersection that was the west end of the boulevard there was a building, a print shop that I had wandered into those years before. I had found that we sahibs were oddly admired there, and the workers would permit us to climb up onto their rooftop three stories above the din because we were, well, export quality. From their roof, two miles of millions spread off on the boulevard beneath as far east as individual humanity could be discerned, then beyond, to the Red Fort. It truly looked like all the people in the world, a single creature comprising millions of cilia, eternally regenerating. We caught our breath, taking in the enormity below, which was less than one tenth of 1 percent of India and thus not the exception on Earth but the rule. We gathered ourselves for retreat—the two miles back to Red Fort and away.

With at least a million others, we had kicked up and breathed a dust of everything that was in the road, much of which was not suitable for kicking, much less breathing. After their first day in India, and that marvelous, disgusting, infuriating initial glimpse of life and disregard in Old Delhi, who wouldn't like a shower? Most in the millions with whom we had wandered would not be satisfied thus anytime soon.

That time fifteen years before, I had been in such crowds in Bombay with Raju, who sold me leather jackets. He told me a bit about how that industry worked, that some of them jumped into vats above their breasts in mortally dangerous tanning chemicals, banned forty years ago everywhere in the West, and stirred hides with their bare bodies, so that, for some others of us, the white skin of cows was turned to burgundy, taupe, chartreuse or mauve. We saw blue and red people walking home. Green people.

As we drove across Bombay, at every stop—and there were plenty—people, obviously under-well, tapped and scraped at the windows for alms. As I rolled the window down to give some pennies, Raju said, "Johnny, what are you doing? You cannot help them all. See how many there are?"

I can help one.

"She does not get to keep anything you give."

The disregarded masses of humanity in India, and those enslaved by absentee advantage takers the world over, by their very lives seem to me to cry out. All the wealth of the world comes from Earth. Ingenuity and labor produce it, but exceptionalism and avarice accumulate it while hundreds of millions stagger, stumble and starve.

How are these hundreds of millions not our concern? Was Raju right? Are we excused our responsibility to our brothers and sisters because there seems too many of them?

What is it to recognize a situation then disregard it? Do we recognize our ignorance of human degradation? Are we even vaguely familiar?

"Cognize," the transitive verb, is "to perceive, to become conscious of, to know." It is included in the verb "recognize": "to acknowledge or accept a specified factual or legal situation, to acknowledge or treat as valid, as existing." It implies looking twice, cognizing, then re-cognizing.

"Ignorance," the noun, is—but is not only—"to not know." It includes the verb "ignore": "to refrain from noticing or recognizing." To ignore is to look twice, also. It is to look at something, and then to look away.

In a world where hundreds of millions of people live in conditions worse than slaves and are denied rights as fundamental as clean water for their infants to drink, where selfish Privateers are encouraged by profits to adopt the absolute minimum of human decency, where imaginary boundaries prevent us from protecting even the clitorises of our little sisters from mutilation in the blasphemous name of some so-called faith, and where government authority is routinely wielded gangster-like by hypocrites trumpeting democracy, freedom, equality, national security, sovereignty and other crocodile values, we stubbornly imagined Goodness was still a thing.

Whatever else our species had learned by my lifetime, there is precious little known about how to fairly execute the founding principles of the United States of America—Liberty and Justice, Equality. Precious less about how to be human or why. What is known is summarily brushed aside as often as other things seem more convenient. And crushed in the press of our crusade to acquire and retain country club comfort for ourselves are all the dreams and cares of the hundreds of millions upon whose misery our comfort depends and who, with us, are all human in the same degree.

As we champion Liberty and Justice, another one of us dies, every four seconds, from hunger. I imagine that, if it is our nature to be sympathetic, this must somehow rub the wrong way.

Perhaps we may henceforth be more ourselves.

9

Our Triumphal Decline to Eden

We have a long way to go on Earth.
It is our burden. But also, it is our fortune.

A GREAT TREE FELL in our forest, Ida, the year you were born. Five big people could not reach around its trunk. I'd love to be standing with you by its stump when you are the age that I am now. Like Kilsli Kaji Sting, your uncle of the great Haida Nation, tells us, the ravens and eagles will still be there, the herons and the other winged ones, the four legs and the swimmers, all will still be there. You won't see me; I would be 130 by then. But there is so much more than eyes can see.

The year your mom and dad were married, we built the Standing Stone Circle with master mason Ron Crawford. Stones, stood up the old way, planted deep in the ground, stand for five thousand years. But instead, we set ours up on concrete foundations. Probably that will be their weakness. For all we know, most concrete will not last even one thousand years. I thought of this after we built them. If they are not pushed over, then, when these stones fall, it will probably be the concrete failing. Still, who knows? Maybe some of that smarty-pants concrete will stand up.

We asked our first guests in the Standing Stone Circle to imagine people there in two hundred years, in 2205. We gave the stones a good chance of standing at least that much longer than us. What would those people know—particularly, about our history? What would they think?

Someone said, "They'll probably wonder what the hell the people *who built these stones* were thinking." Let this book be an answer in part. What we were thinking and what we did about it.

If I am still here with you as you read this, Ida, I won't be for long. After all we have learned, our life expectancy is still less than one hundred years. But my heart swells now, to think of you, of the people you will know (all of you our descendants, yet quite disregarded by us in so many ways) and the things you will see and learn.

We still make the old mistake, attempting to predict the future, though sure as shit off a shovel, *we do not know* now what you will know. Some of the problems that the future will bring are already evident, but their solutions are not. So we consider the problems insoluble because, given only our current tools, they are. But if we could as readily imagine the solutions, the problems would as quickly evaporate. Thus, we try to make predictions about the future without a clue about the inevitable advances and breakthroughs in energy, food production or computing power, and a host of other as yet unimaginable wonders. When English cleric and scholar Thomas Robert Malthus wrote his predictions about population, he could clearly see that increase in production inevitably gave rise to increased population; thus, when faced with Earth's limited capacity, he assumed a catastrophic result. But although he imagined population growth accurately, he was stuck with eighteenth-century technological solutions and could not anticipate our astonishing advances.

Even more, we make our predictions about the future without understanding yet the proper reach of our compassion and of our responsibility. You could easily learn to become better on these accounts than we ever did. I hope very soon we will come to know that bad guys must not be permitted to run wild. Anywhere. We owe it to their victims.

My contemporaries dreamed very big dreams. But even without knowing the disasters you will know, ones that we caused, we have already devastated much of Earth. We presided over the annihilation of many of her species, advanced the demise of countless people exactly like ourselves and permitted the degradation of many hundreds of millions more, all by failing to regard honestly what our society was doing, by failing to live up to the lessons we were taught as children. How much, and whom, will it cost to rid Eden of fossil fuel extraction's toxic fruit?

Joni Mitchell in a radio interview once conceded, "We were going to change the world. When we found out we couldn't do that, then we decided to change ourselves. When we found we couldn't do that either, we decided to get rich." We ran lovely country clubs and congratulated ourselves as successful defenders of Freedom. And for but a moment, we looked out in stunned wonder upon a world full of impoverished people, then we turned our backs. Some of us excused ourselves by saying we must first clean up our own backyards, not realizing there *is* only one backyard.

As for our duty to protect our brothers and sisters from Pricks, though we would be up and armed should it occur within our country club, we acted with utter disregard, it is true. And while innocents were violated abroad, we sang anthems to Freedom and hymns to Sovereignty.

I do not want to dwell upon the countless wrongs already suffered, only upon Kemosabe's obligation to cross the Rio Grande and save the young women of Ciudad Juárez, and of everywhere else. Where we might have elevated ourselves, we have brought the human race down an ugly notch; where we might have accomplished development, we have permitted impoverishment; and where we might have practiced good ecology, we have excused devastation.

Now everybody knows how the lying Pricks of the fossil fuel business pulled the wool over our willing eyes and wreaked devastation upon you, Ida, while trying to get richer at your expense and that of your children. They say we are the ones who got the energy cheaper, and it did help us get around more easily, but *they* are the ones who got billions of dollars in profit. We paid for our energy. Now it's time for them to pay the true costs of their take. A huge portion of those profits derives directly from the willful could-not-care-less degradation of your, Earth's, environment. Those billions, my young friends, are yours. That is how our business should be done properly.

Just 150 years ago, we didn't know what germs were. We have been out of caves only 150 generations, and we think we know just about everything. As we have seen, this is always a laugh. A scream, really.

We think we know our place in a universe that ninety years ago we did not even know existed. Daily, we are confronted by new indications that our maturity as a conscious species has not yet been attained.

With an oblivious shrug, we have gone from a population of 1 billion to 7 billion in your great-grandma's lifetime. Some predict that you will see a leveling off of the population in yours. Soon, we will be 10 billion, and we will do ourselves a great disservice, if, like ExxonMobil, we pretend we did not see the trouble that was coming.

Or worse, if we pretend that . . .

"It's okay because nature will set her own boundaries."

For instance?

"Well, natural limits to food production and clean water."

So, natural solutions like starvation and disease?

"Well, yes. It's natural. It is what happens when there are too many of *them*."

Certainly, if we were Pricks.

There is another way. The sooner we care for each and every one of ourselves, the sooner we may begin the decline of the human population on Earth. We might begin to honor decisions to have no children rather than demean the choice as being selfish. By development and education, we may normalize an average of one- or two-child families. Then we may carry off our long stroll home. It will take time. But, no matter what, something that we can count upon most certainly is that the time *will* come. And go. A hundred years from now exists, as you will surely be able to attest.

I think about 5 billion of us on Earth would be perfect, where we were in 1980, when Bill Evans died and Pink Floyd sang, "We don't need no education." Or even 4 billion, like in 1974, when a newspaper brought down a US president and the Ramones first played CBGB. Six years after my first acid trip.

Once our population begins to decline at 1 percent per year, we will be at those levels again in about three generations. *Your* great-grandchild may be born into that world.

However that may be, it will not emerge until everybody is made safe. We have a long way to go on Earth. It is our burden. But it is also our fortune.

When Adam Smith proposed we each pursue our own self-interest, he presumed we would be primarily sympathetic. If we were more sympathetic than selfish, if we were more dutiful than merely powerful, Eden would be ours and will have been earned.

Then we will be the reason we are here.

"What are we here *for*?"

Exactly, man.

10

All's Well. Where Thou Art Earth and Why

In a single moment of inexplicable realization, we may see that consciousness in the Universe is eternal, that by some miracle we have grown into it and that there is no difference between it and us.

IF WE ARE still inclined to see things the old way, that we are all alone here, 1 in 100,000,000,000,000,000,000,000,000 (100 sextillion) stars, and that we are the sole seed of astounding consciousness anywhere in either infinity or eternity, that is dazzlingly, almost infinitely unlikely. And so, it must be a miracle to be valued beyond literally every-thing that, preposterously, we take for granted, if not utterly disregard, daily.

Another miracle dies, every four seconds, from hunger.

But it takes tremendous imagination and courage to face all likelihood. In all likelihood, we are a few generations away from joining a Universe completely filled with consciousness, which contains knowledge vastly more complete than ours, consciousness that regards goodness, sharing and conservation as bedrock.

Consciousness provides us with the capacity to take in everything that comes our way. The more we know of our Universe and of our place in it, the more there is within ourselves of which to be aware. Consciousness can comprehend the entire Universe so that whatever we discern on our outside may also be awakened within us all.

Consciousness is more or less uniform; only knowledge and experience vary. Knowledge and experience are not consciousness any more than data and code are computing capacity. Consciousness may be affected by knowledge and experience, though when it is, most often it is distracted by them.

That consciousness exists without either knowledge or experience is evident in every infant. An infant human, abandoned and raised by deer, would hardly be the same as a deer and might very well be more conscious than a cousin who became a lawyer and spent their entire life in rumination of facts and law rather than of wild grasses and flowers.

Wherever consciousness occurs in the Universe, it is just as it is here; "more consciousness" is like "more alive." Buddha could not be any more enlightened if he'd meditated a million years more. Nor Jesus more loving. There is no difference between consciousness and love. Yet there is a sum of them; together they equal something astonishing. Consciousness is a capability in us whose marvelousness depends only upon the imagination and courage of its humble, ever so fortunate, host for a time. When we evolve into proper astonishment, it becomes us well.

We seem to be examples of how there came to be consciousness in the Universe. My favorite from the Gospel of Thomas is: "If the flesh came into being because of spirit, it is a wonder. But if spirit came into being because of the body, it is a wonder of wonders. Indeed, I am amazed at how this great wealth has made its home in this poverty" (Thomas, 29). If God created the flesh, that would be a wonder. But if the flesh created consciousness, that would be a wonder of wonders. Again, it is little surprise that these words of Jesus were not embraced by Rome.

"Let him who seeks continue seeking until he finds. When he finds, he will become troubled. When he becomes troubled, he will

be astonished, and he will rule over the All"
(Jesus; Thomas, 2).

Ourselves, and all others alike, are the
Universe's vessels of consciousness. With consciousness comes awareness of responsibility,
and that can be very troubling indeed. But also
there comes astonishment. Perhaps when we
feel that with the most exquisite sensibility,
we do rule over the All.

We may be, after all, the most wonderful
constituents in the Universe, its vessels of consciousness, of astonishment and of love. Every
moment we behave like that is what we are is a
moment of abundance that no amount of money
can increase and of satisfaction that no amount
of power, alone, can ever achieve. So it is no
wonder we feel bad when we behave like we are
something less.

If the whole of the consciousness of us all
in the Universe is greater than the sum of its
parts, then the cumulative consciousness in the
Universe is greater than the sum of some 10 trillion billions of conscious beings. If there is no
thing in the Universe greater than that, it is still
great enough for me. We might have asked Carl
Jung whether he thought there was a collective
conscious. Or Gautama Buddha if he really
meant "All" when he said, "The mind mirror

illumines all ingenuously, the whole Universe a gem of light beyond the terms of in and out."

Or, we may ask ourselves . . . There is no difference.

In a single moment of inexplicable realization, we may see that consciousness in the Universe is eternal, that by some miracle we have grown into it and that there is no difference between it and us. It is the same for us all.

There *is* something "up there" that is infinite and good. It is everything, and it is what we come of. It is what created us, the ones who dream dreams, then make them come real.

So, love Earth, and none the least, love ourselves. All of our selves, including the one in the mirror. It is as easy, and as hard, as just being nice. As we love ourselves, we must protect all from abuse by Pricks. Pricks are ourselves, too, and we must show them the respect of governing them properly, exactly as we show self-respect by governing our selves. Just as we must love ourselves, we must overcome selfishness. By doing so, we will not be hurting anyone, though we may feel we are. We will be healing. Handling Pricks *is* being nice. To everybody.

That will be base camp for the summit of human endeavor, the nurturing and elevation of us all for a million years and beyond, secure in this miracle that has befallen us and to which we will all have attended. Earth will be Eden again, but only when we unfold ourselves upon her that way.

We feel we are instances of consciousness. It comes to us; then we go. But just as we share the collective unconscious described by Carl Jung, we also share consciousness. They are both capacities we all share. We tend to experience our consciousness as individuals, but as individuals we are not the proprietors of consciousness.

If we are not eternal as individuals (though given the vastness of all that we do not yet know, this does seem a considerable "if"), we are, at least, limitless vessels into which pours life's experience. Like wells, we are always full, yet there is always room for more. It doesn't matter how much we are filled, we remain, simply, full.

Wells have water in them, but the water is not something the well creates or owns. Water exists both before the well is created and after it is long gone.

If I were nothing but this well, this vessel that happens to contain consciousness, then there would be an end of me. Consciousness would well up in "me," and then, like old wells do, "I" would crumble.

But we are not the wells; we are the water. We are what wells up. We *are* a heart we all share, that we all feel. It shows what we are. Even if the well were a part of us, it would not be the better part. A well with no water is no well at all. But water needs no well to be.

Now we may well up on Earth for a million years and beyond—if we wish, but still, *only* if we dare.

No, we are not the wells; we are the water. And we will well up in this Universe as long as it's here, the Well of us All.

All's Well.

Pass it on.

"I will. Therefore I am."

Good. Thank you.

The Declaration of Universal Rights and Responsibilities of Freedom

*Just 'cause a b'y's fr'm Newflan' don't
mean he can get 'mself 'shore 'n a rowboat.*

THOMAS O' COMBE BY CHANCE

WHEN IN THE Course of events, it becomes necessary for People to acknowledge and affirm the Responsibilities and Rights that have connected them one with another, and to assume among the People of Earth the separate and equal station to which the Laws of Nature and of Nature's Goodness entitle each of Us, a decent respect for the Good of humankind requires that We declare Our Cause that impels Us to assert the Rights and Responsibilities of Us All so that they be known by All, expected by All, and Accorded to every last one.

We hold these truths to be self-evident, that All People are created equal and that We are All endowed by Creation with certain unalienable Universal Rights. Among these are Life, Liberty and the pursuit of Happiness. They include respect and security of our Person; access to food, clothing and shelter; access to the tools of self-improvement, to health care, to basic capital and to justice; and the Right to a Healthy Environment.

This shall be our duty and our fortune, to accord Universal Rights to All and to do all other Acts and Things required by our Responsibility to All for their Freedom. And for the support of this Declaration, with a firm reliance on the protection of Universal Providence, we mutually pledge to each other our Lives, our Fortunes and our Sacred Honor, so help us Goodness.

ACKNOWLEDGEMENTS

Father Pat O'Byrne for his all-embracing
humanity and Father Dunstan McLellen for his
Francis of Assisi spirit;

Dr. James Black for reciting Shakespeare softly
while pretending to search through the play
for the passage;

Nancy-Jo Cullen for teaching me to honour my
work and to prize poetry above notice; Emily
Schultz for her timely appreciation;

Jane McMullen, Michael and Sandi Greene,
Allan Shewchuck and Pat Blocksom, Geoff and
Lyn Savage, Danny and Ivy Patton, Jim and Enid
Marion for showing how to love on Earth;

Father Joe Toole, Robb Lucy, Carl Graves,
Francis Lynch and the St. Mary's Cathedral boy's
and men's choir for helping sing Palestrina;

Bruce Ramsay, Jeff Proudfoot, Geoff Savage
and many more for exemplary advice that being
a detailed professional must be balanced by
randomness at leisure;

Sam Williams for demonstrating the spirit of
humanity rising above the deck stacked against
many, especially in America;

Padraig, Gail, and all the Cullens and Lefebvres
for excelling as family;

Katharine Armitage Amundson for her courage
and for sharing Emily;

Anne Lefebvre for art above all tribulation
and feeling above all guile;

Ted Lefebvre, my younger brother, for teaching
me manliness, including dancing and crying like
no one is watching;

Jim Hoggan for encouraging me, as a young man,
toward awareness and as an older man, consid-
erate engagement; and

Ida my Muse, Emily my mentor in mindfulness
and elegance, and Hilary my confessor for her
mercy, remission and love, and for her bound-
less faith and encouragement.

See you soon, Dad.

Made in the USA
Columbia, SC
07 February 2020

87658155R00117